Better Homes and Gardens®

1988

CHRISTMAS CRAFTS

© Copyright 1988 by Meredith Corporation, Des Moines, Iowa.
All Rights Reserved. Printed in the United States of America.
First Edition. First Printing.
Library of Congress Catalog Card Number: 87-63205
ISBN: 0-696-01795-4

*Christmas is a time
when all of us take pleasure in the
activities—including handcrafting
decorations and gifts—that give each
family's holiday its own special spirit.
In **1988 Christmas Crafts**, we've
culled the pages of* Better Homes and
Gardens® *magazine and crafts
publications for dozens of trims and
gifts you can make along with new
projects in the techniques and
materials you love. We hope these
ideas and projects will help make this
Christmas the merriest one ever for
you and your loved ones.*

Contents

A Festival of Trees

🎄 The twinkling charm of the Christmas tree makes it the center of our holiday celebrations. In this section you'll find decorated trees that reflect the many moods of Christmas, each laden with ideas for your family's festivities.

The tree of lights, *opposite, is our rendition of the tree that Martin Luther, according to legend, trimmed to make an image of the starry heavens from which Christ had come on Christmas night. (To prevent fire, substitute electric lights for candles on your own tree.) The pyramid tree,* right—*a wooden structure kept from year to year and adorned with branches, apples, nuts, and lights— was a popular German substitute for the woodland tree.*

"'Tis the eve of Christmas, and on our tree gleam candles bright . . . ."

As America expanded its boundaries, the Christmas tree custom traveled westward.

On the frontier, where sophisticated ornaments weren't available, tree decorating was a make-do affair. Dried apples, nuts, cookies, and berries were hung on evergreen branches, opposite. For early settlers, the humblest of ingredients brought joy and sweet fragrance into pioneer dwellings, to create a bit of magic on cold Christmas nights.

On the American prairie, where evergreens were scarce, the pine tree became a handmade stick tree, left. Branches were twined with a few precious greens, and simple, everyday objects hung on its proud little spindles for Christmas Eve.

"At Christmas, play and make good cheer, for Christmas comes but once a year."

"O Christmas tree,
O Christmas tree,
how lovely are thy branches . . . ."

 *The Victorians favored the unabashedly sentimental family tree, lavishly bedecked with candles, ornaments, toys, and—by the 1880s—holiday greetings. The tree* opposite *features reproductions of Victorian cards. A pagan practice of decorating branches with fruit and flowers was translated into the paradise tree to give Christian meaning to the custom. Our version,* above, *is an elegant extension of this tradition.*

Coming Home to Christmas

In everyone's heart and everyone's mind, there's no place like home for Christmas. Families warm and dear, friends old and new, and memories fond and joyous add to our need to be near our roots.

Celebrate the homiest of Christmases by trimming the tree with treasured family ornaments and festive tinsel.

A gold cord garlanding the tree holds greeting cards from friends and loved ones, and a miniature picket fence re-creates a hometown feel. The checkerboard quilt is a variation of a Nine-Patch design. Patchwork star pillows add holiday zest. Instructions for the projects in this section begin on page 18.

Come home to Christmas wherever you are, with gifts and trims reminiscent of childhood, full of joviality and delight. Even Scrooge's heart would melt at the sight of a tree bedecked with toys or a family of goats dressed for the season's most elegant parties.

This goat family, *left,* is so charming that you'll want to display them long past the holiday season. A treasure for children, they're also a perfect gift for almost-grown-up teens or college students and hard-to-please family members. Who, at any age, can resist their rural charm.

Papa and Mama are about 21 inches tall, and Baby measures 18 inches.

Craft them of felt, fake fur, and fabric scraps.

A tiny evergreen becomes a quaint little village with crafts-stick picket fences, toy-train model houses (assembled from kits available at hobby shops), and a child's locomotive underneath. Miniature lights twinkle like stars above this playful "hometown" tree.

Handcrafted accessories individualize our homes, particularly at Christmastime. Choose your favorite colors, fabrics, and yarns for each of these designs, and make your family's holiday the most personal, and warmest, ever.

Display family photos and beloved keepsakes in simple patchwork frames, *right*, that you can make for Christmas giving. The larger frame measures 14½x17 inches; the smaller one is 8 inches square.

Colorful 19-inch-long stockings, *opposite*, knit from scraps, will be chock-full of goodies on Christmas morning. Why not stitch them from remnants left from your handcrafted gifts, as a hint of special treats under the tree.

The cheerful flower-basket design on the fireboard—a welcome suggestion of spring to banish midwinter blahs—is repeated on the matching crewel pillow.

Picket Fence

Shown on page 13.

MATERIALS

Eight ½x¾-inch pine boards, each 44 inches long, for rails
Eight ¼x1⅜-inch pine lattice, each 8 feet long, for fencing
Four 4x4-inch fir posts, each 12½ inches long, for fence posts
1x6-inch pine board, 40 inches long, for tops and bases
4 decorative finials for post tops
1½-inch-long and ½-inch-long finishing nails; screws
Drill; ¼-inch and ½-inch bits
Tracing and graphite papers
Primer
White paint

INSTRUCTIONS

On two adjacent sides of each 4x4-inch fence post, drill and chisel out holes to fit ½x¾-inch rails. The lower holes should be ¾ inch from the bottoms of the posts; the upper holes should be 8 inches from the bottoms of the posts.

Cut the 1x6-inch board into eight 5-inch squares. Using 1½-inch-long finishing nails, secure squares to the bottoms of the posts. Screw the finials to the centers of the remaining squares for the tops; nail the squares to the post tops.

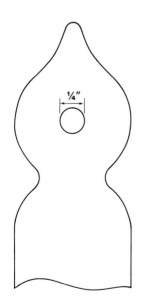

PICKET TOP

For fencing, cut pine lattice into 60 pieces, *each* 12 inches long. Trace pattern for picket top, *below*. Using graphite paper, transfer picket design to tops of lattice pieces. Cut picket pattern; drill a ¼-inch-diameter hole in each piece.

Lay rail pairs 6½ inches apart. Space 15 pieces of fencing 2⅝ inches apart along rails, beginning and ending 2¼ inches from the ends. Let the bottoms of the pieces extend ¾ inch below the bottom rail. Using ½-inch-long finishing nails, secure the fencing in place.

Prime, then paint, the fence and posts white; let dry. To assemble the fence, insert the fence sections into the corner posts.

Checkerboard Quilt

Shown on pages 12 and 13.
The finished quilt is approximately 77x87½ inches.

MATERIALS

4½ yards of white fabric
3½ yards of red print fabric
5½ yards of backing fabric
Cardboard or plastic template material; graph paper
Quilt batting

INSTRUCTIONS

The checkerboard design consists of two quilt-block patterns: A and B. Piece 21 blocks in each pattern.

Template dimensions and all cutting measurements include ¼-inch seam allowances. Sew fabric pieces with *right* sides facing unless directed otherwise. Use ¼-inch seams.

Draw a 4-inch square on graph paper; make a cardboard or plastic template for the square.

From the red fabric, cut two borders, *each* 4x80 inches, and two borders, *each* 4x90 inches.

From the white fabric, cut two borders, *each* 4x80 inches, and two borders, *each* 4x90 inches. Set the borders aside.

TO MAKE BLOCK A: Cut 36 strips, *each* 2¼x26 inches, from both the red and the white fabrics. Sew six strips (three red strips and three

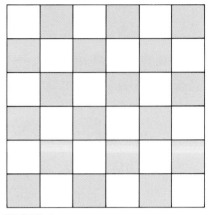

BLOCK A

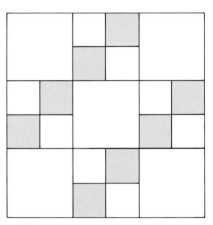

BLOCK B

white strips) together lengthwise, alternating colors. Make 12 sets of strips. Press the seams toward the red fabric.

Cut each strip set crosswise into 11 units of red and white squares, *each* 2¼x11 inches. You will have 132 units altogether; you will use 126 of these.

Sew six units together, alternating placement of the red and white squares, to form one Block A as shown in the diagram, *above*. The finished block should be 10½ inches square, excluding seam allowances. Make 21 of Block A.

TO MAKE BLOCK B: From both the red and the white fabrics, cut nine strips, *each* 2¼x44 inches. From the remaining white fabric, mark and cut 105 squares using the 4-inch-square template.

A	B	A	B	A	B
B	A	B	A	B	A
A	B	A	B	A	B
B	A	B	A	B	A
A	B	A	B	A	B
B	A	B	A	B	A
A	B	A	B	A	B

DIAGRAM OF QUILT TOP

Sew a red and a white strip together, *lengthwise*. Repeat to make nine strip sets.

Cut each strip set crosswise into 19 units of a red and a white square, each 2¼x4 inches. You should have 171 units altogether; you will use 168 of these.

Alternating the placement of the units, join two of the units to make a small red and white checkerboard square. Repeat to make 84 small checkerboard squares. Referring to the diagram, *left,* join white squares and small checked squares to make 21 of Block B. The finished block should be 10½ inches square, excluding seam allowances.

TO ASSEMBLE QUILT TOP: Referring to the diagram, *left,* assemble seven rows of blocks, each row with three of each block pattern. The four odd-number rows begin with Block A. The three even-number rows begin with Block B. Join the rows to make the inner quilt top.

Join pairs of red and white borders *lengthwise*. Sew the 80-inch-long borders to the quilt top and bottom; sew the 90-inch-long borders to the quilt sides. Miter corners.

TO FINISH THE QUILT: Divide the backing fabric into two 99-inch-long pieces. Split one piece *lengthwise* into two pieces; sew narrow pieces onto sides of full panel. Layer quilt top, batting, and backing; baste.

Quilt diagonally through each of the small squares, extending the quilting lines through the large white squares and the borders.

Trim excess batting and backing. Turn in ¼ inch on the quilt top and back. Blindstitch the quilt top to the quilt back to finish the outer edges.

Patchwork Star Pillow

Shown on pages 12 and 13.
The pillow top is 12 inches square.

MATERIALS
1 yard of red print fabric for top, pillow backing, and ruffle
⅛ yard *each* of white print and white solid fabric
13-inch squares of quilt batting and backing fabric
Polyester fiberfill
Water-erasable marking pen
Graph paper; template material

INSTRUCTIONS
Sew all of the fabric pieces with *right* sides facing unless directed otherwise. Use ¼-inch seams.

Trace and make templates for patterns A, B, and C, *below.*

continued

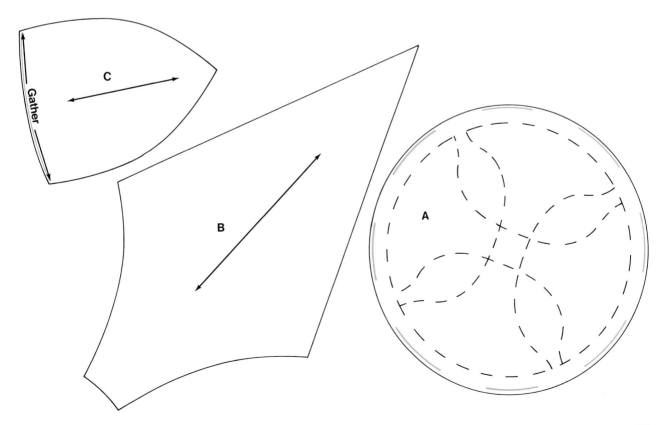

Draw a 3½-inch square on graph paper. Draw a diagonal line, dividing the square into two equal-size triangles. The pattern for template E is the square; the pattern for template D is one triangle. From cardboard or plastic, make templates for D and E. (*Note:* All patterns [A, B, C, D, and E] are finished size; add ¼-inch seam allowances when cutting from fabric.)

TO CUT FABRICS: From the red print fabric, cut two strips, *each* 6x44 inches, for the ruffle. Cut a 12½-inch square for pillow back. Cut one A piece and eight B pieces; add seam allowances. Using a water-erasable pen, copy blue placement markings on the pattern onto piece A.

From the white print fabric, cut eight C pieces and four E pieces. Cut four D pieces with the long side of each triangle on the straight grain of the fabric.

TO PIECE THE PILLOW: Referring to the photograph on pages 12–13, sew eight B and C pieces together to make a star with an open center. Sew the D and E pieces into the outer star edges. Sew gathering thread to *each* C piece on the center seam line (shaded blue on the pattern).

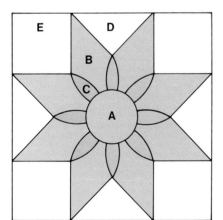

STAR PILLOW DIAGRAM

Sew a gathering thread around the A piece, ⅛ inch outside the seam line (in the seam allowance). Place template A on the *wrong* side of the fabric circle; draw up and tie the gathering thread, bringing the seam allowances to the wrong side. Press; remove template. Appliqué the circle atop the center opening, pulling up gathering threads on C pieces so they match the placement lines indicated on piece A.

TO FINISH THE PILLOW: Press the pillow top. Layer top, batting, and backing; baste together. Hand- or machine-quilt ¼ inch from seams, leaving the C pieces unquilted. A suggested quilting design for piece A is indicated with dashed lines on the pattern.

Sew the ruffle strips into a tube; fold the ruffle in half, *wrong* sides facing, and press. Sew a gathering thread around the ruffle. Pull up the gathering thread to gather a quarter of the ruffle to each pillow side; baste the ruffle to the pillow top.

Sew the pillow back to the pillow top, leaving an opening to turn. Turn right side out, stuff with fiberfill, and hand-sew opening closed.

Picket Fence Tree Garland
Shown on page 15.

MATERIALS
Crafts sticks (available at crafts supply stores)
Fine-gauge wire
White spray paint
Drill

INSTRUCTIONS
Trim 1 inch off ends of crafts sticks. Drill a small hole (centered) in remaining rounded end of each stick for decoration. *Note:* Align several crafts sticks atop one another to make the drilling go faster.

Cut four lengths of wire 15 to 18 inches long. Pair wires, twisting the ends together. Insert a crafts stick between the wires so one pair of wires is near the top of the stick and

one is near the bottom. Twist the wires and insert the next stick. Repeat until the fence is of desired length, adding to wires by twisting on a new length of wire as necessary. Spray-paint the fence white.

Goat Family
Shown on pages 14 and 15.
Adult goats are 21 inches tall; baby goat is 18 inches tall.

MATERIALS
For each goat body
⅝ yard of white fur fabric
2 squares of gray felt for hooves and horns
1 square of white felt for muzzle and insides of ears
2 round, black, shanked buttons (⅝-inch-diameter for adults and ½-inch-diameter for baby)
Black pearl cotton
Powdered rouge
Polyester fiberfill
White carpet thread
Scrap of long-fiber gray fur for Papa's goatee and ear hair
Tracing paper

For clothing
⅜ yard *each* of chintz for Mama's bib and Papa's tie, velveteen for Papa's vest and Baby's collar, gray cotton for Baby's shirt, and mauve cotton for Baby's tie and collar lining and the lining of Papa's vest
⅛ yard of satin
1 yard of 6-inch-wide double-edged lace
1⅛ yards of ¹⁄₁₆-inch-wide ribbon
Three ⅝-inch-diameter silver buttons for Papa's vest
¾ yard of narrow soutache trim
Crafts glue; graph paper

INSTRUCTIONS
Trace patterns for the adult and baby goat on pages 21–26. On graph paper, enlarge patterns for clothing on page 27 to scale. The patterns include ¼-inch seam allowances. Unless directed otherwise, stitch all pieces with *right* sides facing; use ¼-inch seams.

continued

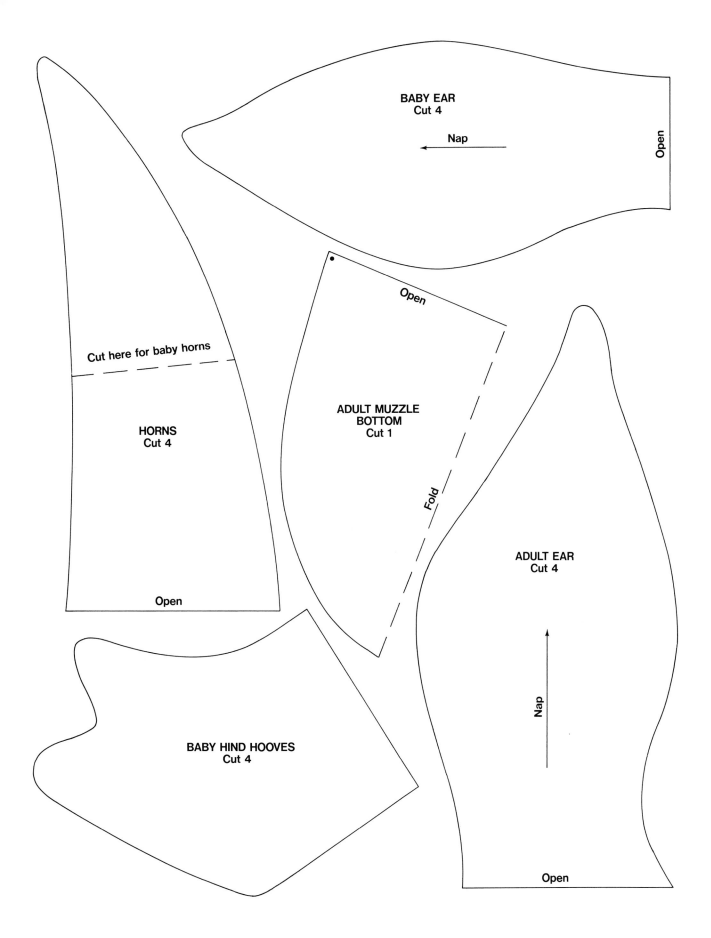

BABY EAR
Cut 4

Nap

Open

Open

Cut here for baby horns

HORNS
Cut 4

ADULT MUZZLE
BOTTOM
Cut 1

Fold

ADULT EAR
Cut 4

Open

Nap

BABY HIND HOOVES
Cut 4

Open

21

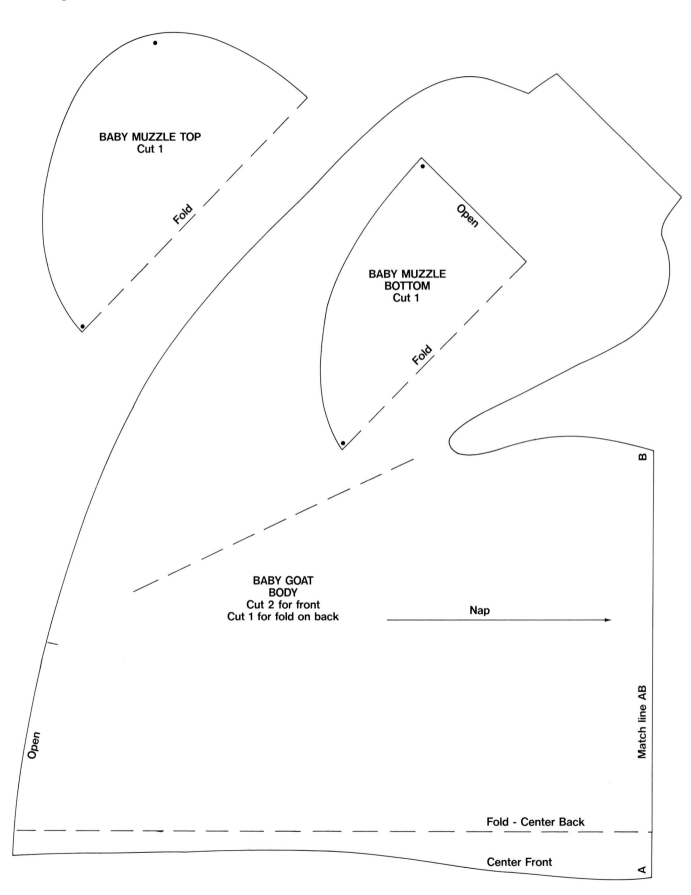

BABY MUZZLE TOP
Cut 1

Fold

BABY MUZZLE
BOTTOM
Cut 1

Open

Fold

BABY GOAT
BODY
Cut 2 for front
Cut 1 for fold on back

Nap

Open

B

Match line AB

Fold - Center Back

Center Front

A

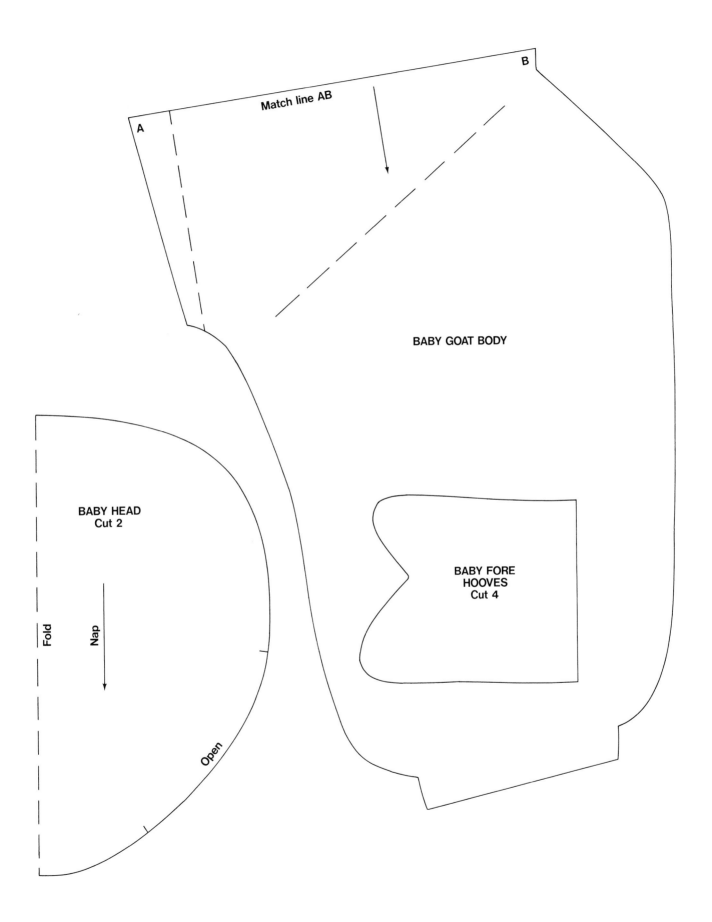

Match line AB

A

B

BABY GOAT BODY

BABY HEAD
Cut 2

Fold

Nap

Open

BABY FORE
HOOVES
Cut 4

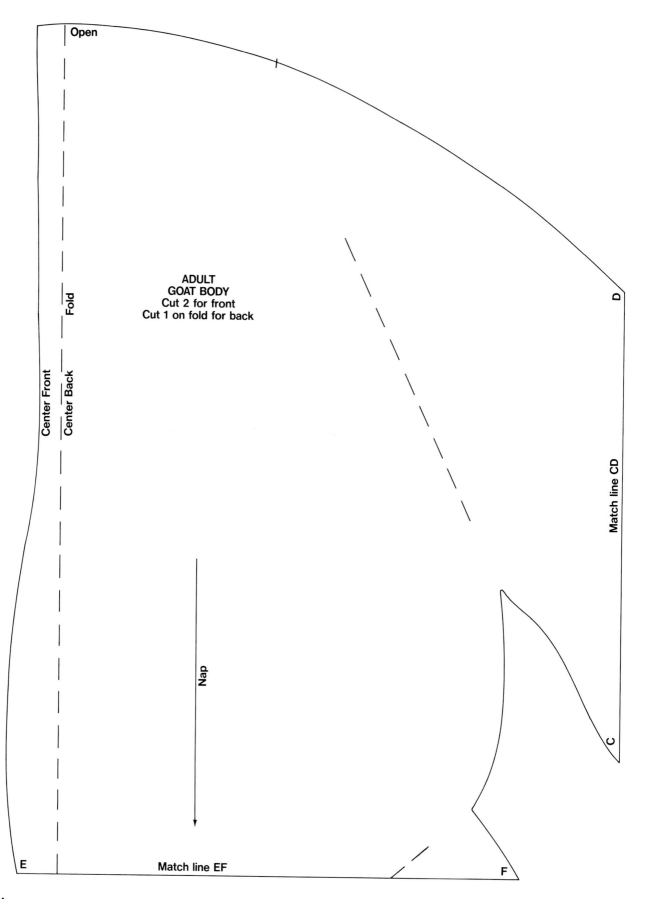

Open

Center Front

Center Back

Fold

ADULT
GOAT BODY
Cut 2 for front
Cut 1 on fold for back

Match line CD

D

C

Nap

E

Match line EF

F

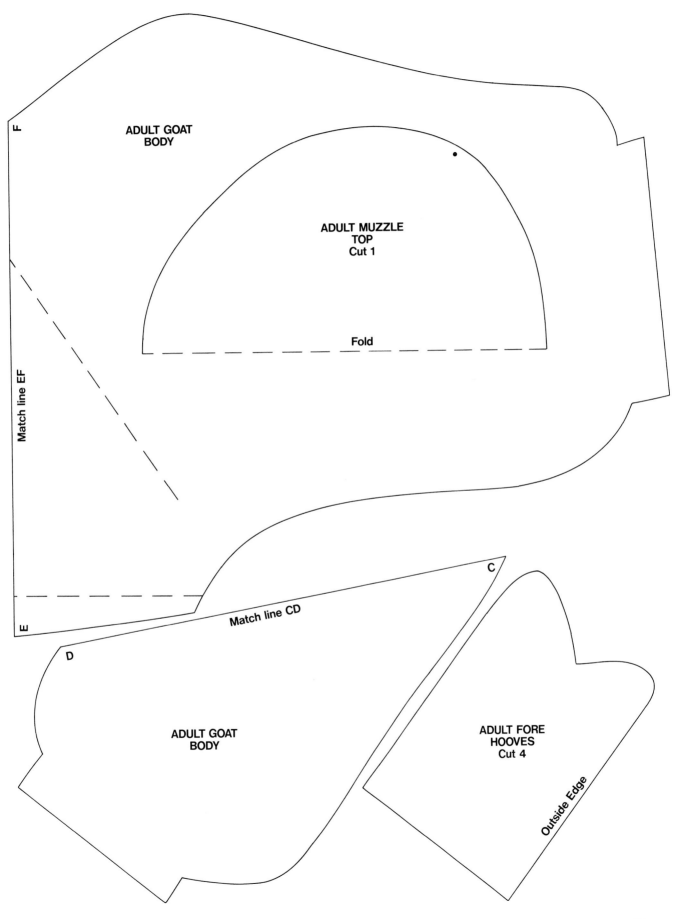

ADULT GOAT
BODY

F

ADULT MUZZLE
TOP
Cut 1

•

Fold

Match line EF

E

D

Match line CD

C

ADULT GOAT
BODY

ADULT FORE
HOOVES
Cut 4

Outside Edge

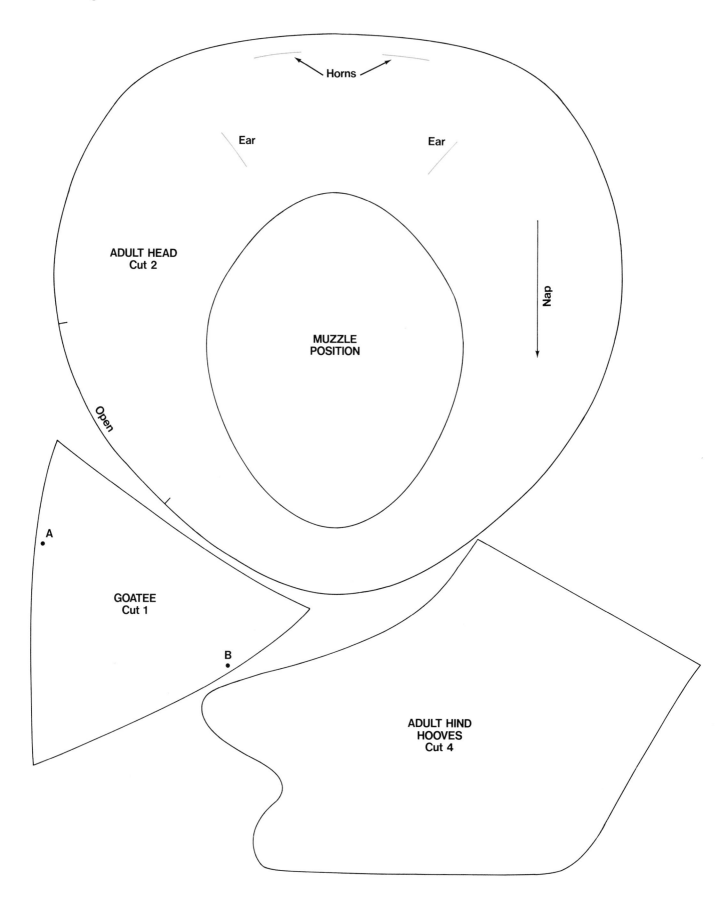

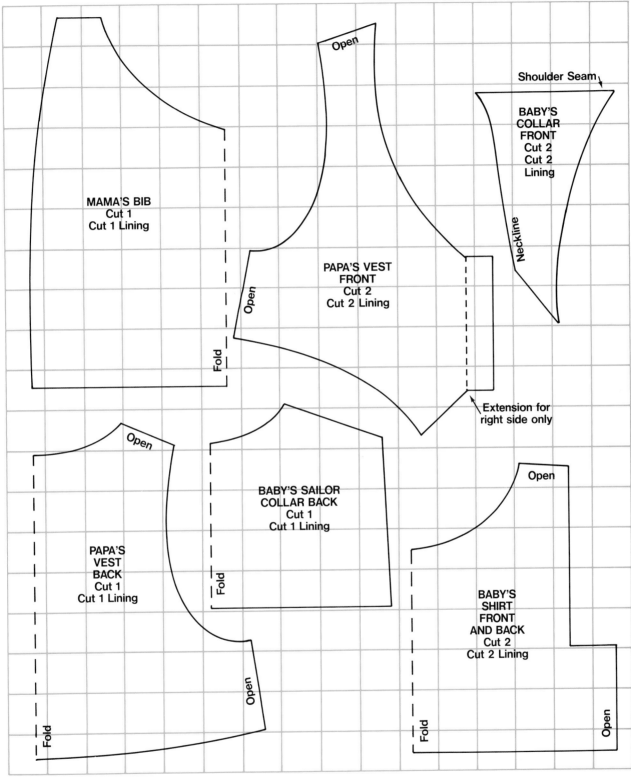

MAMA'S BIB
Cut 1
Cut 1 Lining

Open

PAPA'S VEST
FRONT
Cut 2
Cut 2 Lining

Fold

Open

Shoulder Seam

BABY'S
COLLAR
FRONT
Cut 2
Cut 2
Lining

Neckline

Extension for
right side only

Open

PAPA'S
VEST
BACK
Cut 1
Cut 1 Lining

Fold

BABY'S SAILOR
COLLAR BACK
Cut 1
Cut 1 Lining

Fold

Open

Open

BABY'S
SHIRT
FRONT
AND BACK
Cut 2
Cut 2 Lining

Fold

Open

1 Square = 1 Inch

For *each* goat, cut the following pieces from white fur: one body back and two *each* of ears, head, and body front, reversing direction of one body front.

From the white felt, cut one *each* of lower muzzle and upper muzzle; cut two ears slightly larger than the pattern piece. From the gray felt, cut four *each* of horns, fore hooves, and hind hooves. From the gray fur, cut one goatee.

Sew fronts along the center front seam. Sew fore and hind hooves to ends of legs. Sew front to back, leaving neck open between marks. Clip curves; turn right side out. Stuff all hooves and legs. With carpet thread, hand-sew across all legs along dotted lines. Stuff remainder of body; slip-stitch closed.

HEAD: Sew front to back, leaving seam open between marks. Clip curves; turn; stuff. Stitch closed.

Sew muzzle top to muzzle bottom, leaving open between dots. Clip, turn, and stuff. Place muzzle atop head; whipstitch in place. Using a double strand of pearl cotton, stitch a mouth on the muzzle. Sew on eyes 1 inch above the muzzle.

Sew felt ears to fur ears with edges even. Clip and turn. Tack edges together on the felt side of ears to create a curved shape. Sew ears to head using carpet thread.

For Mama, blush cheeks and ears with powdered rouge. For Papa, cut narrow strips of gray fur for ear hair and glue at the top of the ears. For the goatee, whipstitch sides A and B together, *right* sides out. Stitch in place with the seam to the back.

Sew horns together. Trim excess; turn and stuff. Turn raw edges under ¼ inch; stitch to head. Tuck bottom half of head into body opening. Sew head to body, using double strand of carpet thread.

MAMA'S CLOTHES: From chintz cut pieces as follows: two bibs, one 3½x30-inch strip for bib ruffle, and two ties, *each* 3½x22 inches.

With right sides facing, fold each tie in half *lengthwise*. Sew across one end and along the long edge; turn and press. Stitch the raw edge of the ties to the shoulders of the bib, pleating the tie to fit.

Pin bib lining to bib front, allowing ties to hang out bottom. Sew bib to lining, leaving bottom edge unsewn. Clip, turn, and press.

Narrowly hem ruffle ends and long edge. Gather ruffle to bottom edge of the bib front *only*. Turn under raw edge of lining; slip-stitch over raw edge of ruffle.

Cut a satin sash 3½x44 inches. Fold the sash in half *lengthwise*; stitch across one end and along long edge, leaving an opening for turning. Turn and press; sew opening closed.

Fold sash in half, *crosswise,* to determine the center. Tack sash center to the left side seam of bib.

Tie the bib to Mama at the neckline. Tie the sash at the waist.

For the lace collar, place the ribbon down the center of the lace. Zigzag over the ribbon using a wide stitch to form a casing. *Note:* Do not catch the edge of the ribbon in the stitching. Pull up the lace along the ribbon to gather the collar; tie the collar around Mama's neck. If desired, tack a ribbon rosette to the head between the ears.

PAPA'S CLOTHES: From the velveteen and the mauve cotton fabrics, cut two vest fronts and one vest back. From the velveteen, cut two 2½x2¾-inch pieces for pockets. From chintz, cut one 3x20-inch rectangle for a bow tie.

Sew lining to vest back along neck, armhole, and bottom edges, stopping ¼ inch from the shoulder and side edges. Sew lining to fronts along neck, front, bottom, and armhole edges, stopping ¼ inch from the shoulder and side edges.

Pinning the lining out of the way, join the fronts to the back at the shoulder seams. Then blindstitch the lining over the seam, turning under the raw edge of lining. Sew the side seams in the same manner.

With right sides facing, fold pocket flaps in half; stitch across ends and along long edge, leaving opening for turning. Turn; sew opening closed and press. Hand-sew pocket flaps onto the vest. Overlap vest fronts and sew on the silver buttons.

With right sides facing, fold the tie in half *lengthwise;* stitch, leaving an opening for turning. Turn and press. Sew opening closed; tie in a bow and tack under Papa's chin.

BABY'S CLOTHES: From gray cotton fabric, cut four of baby's shirt for the shirt and lining. Cut one collar back and two collar fronts *each* from velveteen and mauve cotton fabrics. Cut a 4×15½-inch strip of mauve cotton fabric for the tie.

Sew the shirt back to the lining in the same manner as for Papa's vest back. Repeat for the shirt front. Join the front and back at one side seam. Place the shirt on the goat. Overlap the open side to fit the goat. Hand-sew the side seam of the lining; turn under the raw edges of the shirt front and blindstitch in place.

Sew the collar fronts to the collar back at the shoulders. Repeat for the collar lining. Sew the lining to the collar, leaving an opening for turning. Clip and turn. Sew the opening closed and press. Glue braid around collar, ¼ inch from the collar edge. Slip the collar around Baby's neck and tack the collar to the shirt front.

Fold tie in half *lengthwise;* sew across ends and along long edge, leaving an opening. Turn; sew opening closed, and press. Tie a knot in center; tack to bottom of collar.

Patchwork Frames
Shown on page 16.
The large frame is 14½x17 inches; the small frame is 8 inches square.

MATERIALS
For the large frame
½ yard of green print fabric
¼ yard of beige print fabric
¾ yard of muslin
½ yard of 1-inch-thick polyester batting; two 14½x17-inch pieces of cardboard

For the small frame
¼ yard *each* of green print and beige print fabrics; ⅓ yard of muslin

¼ yard of 1-inch-thick polyester batting

Two 8x8-inch pieces of cardboard

For both frames
Graph paper; mat knife

Cardboard or plastic for templates

Scraps of blue print and brown print fabrics

Water-erasable marking pen

Masking tape; crafts glue

INSTRUCTIONS
Measurements for templates and fabric pieces include ¼-inch seam margins. Sew pieces with *right* sides facing unless directed otherwise.

For the large frame
Draw a 1½-inch square on graph paper. Make a template from plastic or cardboard. On brown print, use template to mark 16 squares. Mark 20 squares on blue print. Cut out squares; set aside.

From the green print fabric, cut four 1½ × 11½-inch strips and four 1½ × 9-inch strips. From the beige print fabric, cut two 1½ × 11½-inch strips and two 1½ × 9-inch strips.

From the muslin, cut two 3 × 17-inch strips and two 3 × 14½-inch strips. Cut one 14½x17-inch rectangle for the facing.

TO PIECE THE FRAME: Join four brown squares and five blue squares to form a checkerboard; press. Repeat three times; set aside.

Sew a green strip to *each* long edge of the beige print strips. Press the seams toward the green strips.

Sew a pieced square to both ends of the two long green and beige pieces. Sew short green and beige pieces to each pieced square, forming a rectangle.

Sew muslin strips to the outer edges of the frame. Press under ¼ inch on outer edges of muslin strips.

Pin the pieced frame to the muslin rectangle, *right* sides together. Sew around the center opening. Slit the muslin center from corner to corner diagonally and trim excess muslin from the center opening. Pull the muslin through the center opening to turn right side out.

Using a mat knife, cut an 8½x11-inch rectangle from the center of one large cardboard piece.

TO ASSEMBLE THE FRAME: Glue several layers of batting to the cardboard frame to form a thick pad.

Slip the padded cardboard between the top and the lining, pulling the lining through to the frame back and the pieced fabric to frame front. Secure edges of the muslin rectangle to the frame back with tape and glue, making sure the center seams are aligned with the frame opening.

Stretch pieced fabric over frame front, pulling outer muslin strips to frame back. Make sure pieced fabric is smooth and even on frame front. Tape the muslin strips to frame back, mitering corners and tucking under raw edges; whipstitch to muslin rectangle on frame back.

Cut remaining cardboard slightly smaller than frame. Tape picture on cardboard. Cut muslin ½ inch larger on all sides than cardboard. Glue fabric to cardboard back; turn under raw edges. Whipstitch cardboard to frame back.

For the small frame
Draw a 1-inch square on graph paper; make cardboard or plastic template. On brown print fabric, use the template to mark 16 squares. Mark 20 squares on blue print fabric. Cut out squares; set aside.

Cut eight 1x5½-inch strips from the green fabric; cut four 1x5½-inch strips from the beige print fabric. From the muslin, cut four 1¾x8-inch strips and one 8-inch square.

With a mat knife, cut a square 5x5 inches in the center of one cardboard piece.

Refer to the instructions for the large frame, above, to piece and assemble the small frame.

Knit Stockings
Shown on page 17.
Finished stocking is 19 inches long.

MATERIALS
Size 7 sixteen-inch circular knitting needle

Size 8 sixteen-inch circular knitting needle

1 set of Size 8 double-pointed knitting needles

Scraps of acrylic yarn

Stitch markers; tapestry needle

Gauge: 5 sts = 1 inch

continued

KNITTING ABBREVIATIONS

beg	begin(ning)	rnd	round
dec	decrease	sk	skip
dp	double pointed	sl st	slip stitch
grp	group	sp	space
inc	increase	st(s)	stitch(es)
k	knit	st st	stockinette stitch
lp(s)	loop(s)	tog	together
MC	main color	yo	yarn over
p	purl	*....repeat from * as indicated	
pat	pattern	( )..........repeat between ( ) as indicated	
psso	pass slip st over		
rem	remaining	[ ]..........repeat between [ ] as indicated	
rep	repeat		

FIRE BOARD 1 Square = 3 Inches

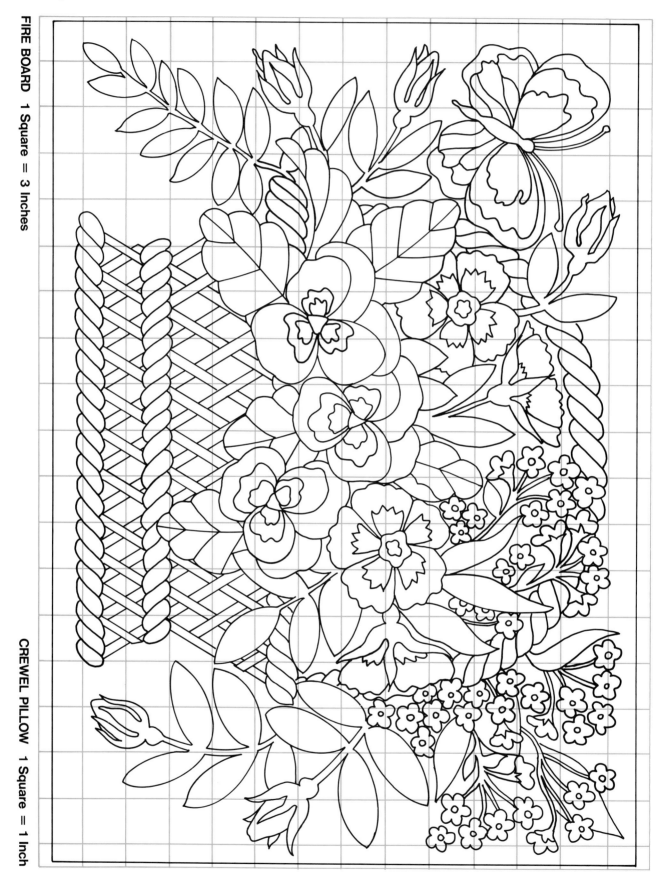

CREWEL PILLOW 1 Square = 1 Inch

INSTRUCTIONS

The stockings shown in the photograph on page 17 feature stripes made by working a color for two rounds. To make the most of your yarn scraps, establish your own stripe sequence or knit random-width stripes.

BODY: Starting at top with Size 7 circular needle, cast on 60 sts and join. Place marker for beg of round to mark center back of stocking. Work in k 1, p 1 ribbing for 1¼ inches. Change to Size 8 circular needle. Work in a stripe pattern of two or more rounds of each color. Repeat the stripe sequence or continue to add new colors until the piece measures 11 inches.

HEEL: With the same yarn color as the last stripe, k 15 sts, place marker, turn; p back 30 sts, place marker, turn; k 29 sts, turn; p 28 sts, turn; k 27 sts, turn; p 26 sts, turn. Continue in this manner until there are 8 sts remaining (4 sts on each side of center back of round marker). End after a purl row.

Turn; k 9, turn; p 10, turn; k 11, turn; p 12, turn; k 13, turn; continue in the same manner until all 30 sts of the heel have been worked; on the last purl row, purl 15 (to the center back of the heel marker).

Break off yarn. With the next color, turn and begin working in full rounds, removing heel markers.

Work even in rounds, changing color every 2 rounds or according to your stripe sequence until the piece measures 6½ inches in from end of heel. End after a complete stripe.

TOE: K next round in the next color. Continue with the same color for the entire toe. Divide sts onto double-pointed needles.

Dec Rnd 1: * K 12, k 2 tog, k 2, slip 1, k 1, psso, k 12, repeat from *.

Rnd 2 and all other even-numbered rounds: Knit.

Dec Rnd 2: * K 11, k 2 tog, k 2, slip 1, k 1, psso, k 11; repeat from *.

Dec Rnd 3: * K 10, k 2 tog, k 2, slip 1, k 1, psso, k 10; repeat from *.

Continue the decrease pattern until there are 20 sts on the needles. End after an even round.

Knit the first 5 sts, put the next 10 sts on one needle without working them, put the last 5 sts on the first needle with the other 5 sts.

Weave the toe of the stocking together. Weave in all yarn ends; steam the finished stocking very lightly to block.

Crewel Pillow
Shown on page 17.
Pillow is 18x24 inches.

MATERIALS
18x24-inch piece of green wool
Purple, light purple, pink, light pink, yellow, light yellow, light blue, black, white, brown, gold, gray, dark green, green, and light green 3-ply Persian yarn
1 yard of cotton fabric for ruffle and pillow back
2½ yards of contrasting piping
Graph paper
Polyester fiberfill

INSTRUCTIONS
Enlarge the pattern on page 30 onto graph paper; transfer the design to wool piece.

Refer to photograph for yarn colors. Use one yarn strand to satin-stitch flowers, leaves, and butterfly. Work rosebuds in long-and-short stitches and forget-me-nots in lazy daisy stitches with French-knot centers and chain-stitch stems. Back-stitch flower and leaf stems.

For woven basket sections, twist six yarn strands; couch at crossings. Satin-stitch solid basket sections; outline with backstitches.

When embroidery is completed, block the pillow top with a medium-hot iron and a damp press cloth.

From cotton fabric, cut an 18x24-inch pillow back and four 7x44-inch ruffles. Baste piping to pillow front.

Stitch ruffle; baste to pillow front. Sew pillow front to back, leaving an opening. Clip, turn, and stuff. Stitch opening closed.

Fireboard
Shown on page 17.

MATERIALS
Random widths of 1-inch pine lumber to cover fireplace opening
11/16x3¼-inch bed molding to frame the painted design
1x2-inch boards for back bracing
Graph paper
Graphite paper
Paint in the following colors: dark green, green, purple, pink, white, brown, and gold
1¼-inch-long finishing nails
Wood screws, 1¼ inches long
Paintbrush and artist's brushes
Permanent black marker for outlines
Clear acrylic spray

INSTRUCTIONS
Measure the fireplace opening. Plan the fireboard to exceed the fireplace opening by about 2 to 3 inches at the top and sides. Cut pine boards to desired length, laying them side by side to achieve necessary height.

Cut three 1x2-inch back braces to span the boards and place on the back side of the fireboard, perpendicular to the board joints. Screw the braces to the boards, placing one brace in the center and the others at the ends.

Paint fireboard dark green. Cut bed molding to form a frame for the fireboard front, mitering the corners. Paint the molding brown.

Enlarge the pattern, *opposite,* onto graph paper. Transfer pattern to fireboard with graphite paper.

Refer to photograph for colors, or paint design as desired. Outline the designs with a permanent felt-tip marker. Nail molding atop the fireboard. Spray with clear acrylic.

Stand the fireboard in front of the firebox opening when the fireplace is not in use.

Down-Home Christmas on the Farm

For many of us, Christmas means a return to the family farmstead and the cheer of its kitchen. It's a wonderful place to indulge our love of old-fashioned pleasures—stringing popcorn balls with Grandma, baking cookies and holiday breads (Ah, the spectacular smells of Christmas!), and trimming a special tree in tribute to down-on-the-farm simplicity.

Children and grandparents enjoy the togetherness of making simple ornaments such as tiny popcorn-ball garlands for the tree. Ginger cookies, candied citrus peel, and dried-apple wreaths garnish the tree. Underneath are a "snowflake in the trees" place mat, stitched from prequilted fabrics and colorful trims, and bright rag baskets to fill with food gifts and other holiday treasures.

Instructions for all of the projects in this section begin on page 40.

You needn't can your own homegrown fruits and vegetables or put up jars and jars of homemade jam to create the aura of a back-to-basics farm Christmas. Instead, make colorful rag baskets for family members and friends—and fill them with home-baked gifts.

Or, core crisp apples and place candles in the centers to form cheery decorations. Put one of them on a barbed-wire wreath with greens for hanging in a window.

Make charming apple wreaths by stringing dried apples on wire. Purchase dried apples, or dry them at home.

Homemade goodies and handcrafted decorations are hallmarks of a country holiday. To capture the magic of Christmas on the farm at your house, craft country-style trims from everyday things. Ginger cookies, popcorn balls, fresh or dried apples, and barbed wire wrapped into a wreath create an atmosphere of rural celebration even in the city.

The Shaker-style grandfather clock, doll high chair, and child-size cupboard, *left,* are perfect for playing house. Built of pine, they'll be cherished for years to come.

For the tree, *left,* piece two diminutive star patterns into tiny "quilts." Make rag ornaments, *right,* by wrapping plastic foam balls with narrow strips of fabric.

For lace-trimmed ornaments, have a photo shop duplicate old snapshots from the family album. Mount photos on cardboard and embellish them with elegant edgings.

Share the special spirit of a farm Christmas by trimming the tree with miniature patchwork quilts, rag-wrapped balls, and old family photos edged in lace. Simply designed doll furniture, such as the three pieces shown here, will warm the hearts of your children (or grandchildren) and provide lots of practical storage for their playthings.

Doll clothes and tiny quilts pinned to a tree make an unexpected decoration for a child's room or any empty corner. (These 4½-inch-square quilts are similar to those on the large tree on page 36.)

To outfit your children's dolls, use a favorite pattern, and give the clothes to children during the holidays.

What young miss wouldn't be delighted with a rosy-cheeked, huggable doll—a welcome gift at any time—and her own collection of doll quilts based on Amish designs. For another pleasant surprise, trim a tiny tree with doll clothes and ornament-size patchwork coverlets.

Stitch a homespun look-alike for the kids on your list. Match the hair and clothing of this huggable country doll, *opposite,* to your favorite child for an extra-special look this Christmas.

A basket full of vivid doll-size quilts (26½ inches square and 26½x30 inches) will spark any child's imagination. And after comforting many a doll through the years, the bright quilts can be used as decorative wall hangings. Well-loved traditional country designs and colors inspire each of the four patterns.

Popcorn-Ball Garlands

Shown on pages 32 and 33.

INGREDIENTS
10 cups popped popcorn (about ½
  cup unpopped)
1 cup sugar
¼ cup light corn syrup
½ teaspoon vinegar
¼ teaspoon salt
¾ cup water
½ teaspoon vanilla
Red ribbon

INSTRUCTIONS
Note: Because the ribbon may contain nonedible dye, use the balls with ribbon for decoration only and not for eating. Popcorn balls without ribbon are edible.

Remove all of the unpopped kernels from the popcorn. Put the popcorn in a large baking pan; keep it warm in a 300° oven.

Butter the sides of a heavy 1-quart saucepan. In the saucepan, combine the sugar, corn syrup, vinegar, salt, and water. Cook over medium-high heat to boiling, stirring constantly with a wooden spoon to dissolve the sugar. Avoid splashing the mixture on the sides of the pan. Clip a candy thermometer to the side of the pan.

Cook, stirring occasionally, until the thermometer registers 270° (soft-crack stage). The mixture should boil at a moderate, steady rate over the entire surface. It will take 30 to 35 minutes to dissolve the sugar and reach the soft-crack stage.

Remove from the heat; stir in the vanilla. Slowly pour the mixture evenly over hot popcorn. Stir just until mixed. Working quickly, scoop up small amounts of popcorn mixture with buttered hands. Shape mixture into 1- to 1½-inch balls, forming the balls at 2- to 3-inch intervals along a piece of ribbon.

For ornaments, form 1½- to 3-inch-diameter balls. Tuck both ends of a 6-inch piece of ribbon into each ball at the same spot, creating a loop for hanging. Makes about twenty 1- to 1½-inch balls or eight to ten 3-inch balls.

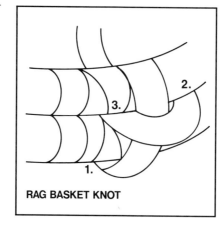

RAG BASKET KNOT

Rag Basket

Shown on pages 32 and 33.
Finished basket is approximately 12 inches in diameter.

MATERIALS
12 yards of paper core roping, available at crafts and weaving stores
Approximately 3 yards total of scrap fabrics in assorted colors
Large rug needle

INSTRUCTIONS
Tear or cut the fabrics into 2-inch-wide strips. At one end of the roping, begin wrapping a fabric strip around the roping. Coil the roping into a flat disk as you wrap.

Use the wrapping strip to tie the coils together at the beginning and at 2-inch intervals as you work. To tie, refer to the diagram, *above,* and follow the instructions below.

To tie, thread the fabric strip into the needle, then wrap the fabric strip from outer row to inner row on the outside of the coil (1).

Next, use the needle to thread the fabric strip between the coils, coming from the back to the front on the right-hand side of the knot (2).

Pull the strip tight and thread it to the inside of the coil, to the left of the knot (3). Pull the strip tight and continue wrapping the outer row. The knot should be on the outside.

To add a new fabric strip, wrap over the end of the old strip (with the new strip) about four times. Continue coiling the roping to form a 7-inch-diameter circle for the bottom of the basket.

Build the basket walls by gradually curving the additional rows to form a bowl shape.

To end, wrap the top row to the previous row for 2 inches, using the needle to thread the strip between the rows. Thread the end of the fabric strip back through the wrapping, and trim the end.

Apple Wreaths

Shown on pages 33 and 35.
Wreaths are approximately 5 inches in diameter.

MATERIALS
Dried apple slices (purchased, or dried following directions below)
One 14-inch piece of medium-weight wire for each wreath
Scrap of solid red cotton fabric
Ascorbic-acid color-keeper (if drying your own apples)

INSTRUCTIONS
To dry your own apples
Choose firm, ripe apples. Cut apples evenly into ⅛-inch-thick slices or rings.

Prepare ascorbic-acid color-keeper according to package directions. Soak the apple slices in the solution about 5 minutes. Drain and pat dry.

Arrange the slices one layer deep on wire cooling racks. Following the manufacturer's directions, dry in a food dehydrator or in a convection oven. Or, dry in a 150° to 200° conventional oven for 1 to 2 hours, rotating cooling racks several times and turning the apples. Cool.

To make the wreaths
String the apple slices onto wire. Shape wire into a circle; twist ends together to fasten. Tear red fabric into a 1-inch-wide strip; tie in a bow at the top of the wreath.

Snowflake Place Mats

Shown on pages 32 and 33.
Place mats are 17 inches in diameter.

MATERIALS

1 yard *each* of prequilted fabric and backing fabric
⅜ yard *each* of green and blue-green fabrics
2 yards of tear-away interfacing
½ yard of fabric for bias binding or 6 yards of bias tape

INSTRUCTIONS

Cut four circles, *each* 17 inches in diameter, from the quilted fabric, the backing fabric, and the interfacing (12 circles total). Trace tree pattern, *below*. Cut 16 trees *each* from the green and blue-green fabrics.

Baste the interfacing to the wrong side of the quilted circles. Place four trees of each color in a circle on each place mat, alternating colors. The bottom branches should touch and the tops should be approximately 2¼ inches from the center. Machine-appliqué trees in place using a narrow zigzag stitch. Trim or tear away excess interfacing.

Baste the backing fabric to the top, *wrong* sides together. Trim the edges evenly.

Machine-quilt ⅛ inch from the inner and outer edges of the trees. Bind the edges of the place mats with contrasting bias tape.

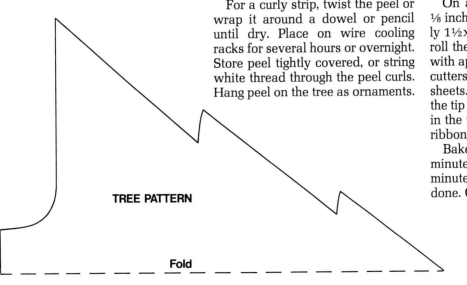

TREE PATTERN

Fold

Candied Citrus Peel

Shown on page 33.
Recipe yields about 4 cups of candied peel.

INGREDIENTS

2 large grapefruits or 4 large oranges
1½ cups sugar
¾ cup water
Sugar

INSTRUCTIONS

Using the point of a sharp paring knife, score each grapefruit or orange peel lengthwise into four sections. Loosen the peel from the fruit, leaving the white pith membrane attached to the peel.

Place the peel in a 3-quart saucepan. Add water to cover the peel. Bring to boiling. Remove from the heat. Let stand for 10 minutes; drain off the water. Repeat the boiling, standing, and draining processes three times, using fresh water each time. Cool the peel.

Cut the peel into strips 4 to 5 inches long and ⅛ to ¼ inch wide. In a saucepan, combine the sugar and ¾ cup water. Bring to boiling, stirring to dissolve the sugar. Add the peel. Cook the mixture over medium heat, stirring occasionally, for 20 to 25 minutes or until peel is translucent. Drain thoroughly; cool for 20 minutes or until lukewarm. Roll the peel strips in sugar.

For a curly strip, twist the peel or wrap it around a dowel or pencil until dry. Place on wire cooling racks for several hours or overnight. Store peel tightly covered, or string white thread through the peel curls. Hang peel on the tree as ornaments.

Ginger Cookies

Shown on pages 33 and 34.
Recipe makes about 72 small cookies or 6 large ones.

INGREDIENTS

3 cups all-purpose flour
1 cup whole wheat flour
2 teaspoons ground cinnamon
1 teaspoon ground ginger
½ teaspoon baking soda
1 cup butter or margarine
1 cup packed brown sugar
⅓ cup molasses
1 egg
1 tablespoon finely shredded orange peel
2 tablespoons orange juice
1 recipe Powdered Sugar Icing
Raisins or small, round, colored candies (optional)

INSTRUCTIONS

In a medium mixing bowl, stir together flours, cinnamon, ginger, and baking soda. Set aside.

In a large mixer bowl, beat the butter or margarine with an electric mixer on medium speed for 30 seconds. Add the brown sugar and beat until fluffy. Add molasses, egg, orange peel, and orange juice; beat well. Gradually beat in flour mixture, stirring in the last of it with a wooden spoon.

Divide the dough in half. Cover and chill about 1 hour or until dough is no longer sticky.

On a floured surface, roll dough ⅛ inch thick. Cut with approximately 1½x4½-inch cookie cutters. (Or, roll the dough ¼ inch thick and cut with approximately 5x9-inch cookie cutters.) Place on ungreased cookie sheets. With the end of a straw or the tip of a paring knife, make a hole in the top of each cookie to insert a ribbon to hang the cookie.

Bake in a 375° oven for 8 to 10 minutes for small cookies, 18 to 20 minutes for large cookies, or until done. Cool cookies on a wire rack.
continued

To decorate cookies, pipe Powdered Sugar Icing onto the cookies with a decorating bag and a writing tip. Add raisins or candies for eyes, buttons, and trims on cookies.

String thread through the hole in each cookie and tie to make a hanging loop.

POWDERED SUGAR ICING: In a medium mixing bowl, stir together 2 cups sifted powdered sugar, ½ teaspoon vanilla, and enough milk (2 to 3 tablespoons) to make a frosting of piping consistency.

Makes about ½ cup frosting. *Note:* Depending on how generously you decorate the cookies, you may need to double the icing recipe.

Barbed-Wire Wreath

Shown on page 34.
Finished wreath is approximately 14 inches in diameter.

MATERIALS

5 yards of barbed wire
Medium-weight wire
Large red apple
Candle
Evergreen branches
Pliers
Wire cutters
Apple corer
Heavy gloves

INSTRUCTIONS

Wearing heavy gloves to protect your hands, coil the barbed wire into a 14-inch-diameter circle. Cut six 10-inch pieces of the medium-weight wire. Use the wire pieces to fasten the barbed wire at intervals around wreath. Trim excess wire pieces with the wire cutters.

Using an apple corer, cut out the apple center to fit the candle. Insert the candle in the apple.

Wire evergreen branches to the wreath and nestle the apple within the branches.

Rag Ball Ornaments

Shown on pages 36 and 37.
Finished ornaments are 3 inches in diameter.

MATERIALS

3-inch-diameter plastic foam balls
Assorted cotton fabric scraps
Hairpins
Straight pins
Heavy thread or string

INSTRUCTIONS

Tear the fabric scraps into 1-inch-wide strips. Wrap a strip around the ball, securing the ends with straight pins. Add additional strips until the ball is covered.

When the ball is covered, insert a hairpin at the top. Insert thread or string through the hairpin and tie to form a hanging loop.

If desired, tie a fabric strip into a bow or tie a length of ribbon into a bow. Pin the bow atop the ball.

Lace-Trimmed Photographs

Shown on pages 36 and 37.

MATERIALS

Photographs
Scraps of lace or small crocheted doilies
Rubber cement
Poster board or lightweight cardboard
Crafts glue
Heavy thread or string

INSTRUCTIONS

Using rubber cement, affix a photograph to poster board. Measure and cut lace to trim the edges of the photograph. Glue the lace around the photograph perimeter. If using a doily, center the photograph on the doily; glue. Insert thread or string through a hole in the lace and tie into a loop.

Doll's High Chair

Shown on pages 37 and 38.
Finished chair is 23½ inches tall.

MATERIALS

Wood as listed in the materials chart, *below.*
8 yards of 1-inch-wide cloth strips
1½-inch-long finishing nails
Drill; ¾-inch bit
Wood glue; wood putty
Sandpaper; varnish or sealer

MATERIALS			
Part	Finished Size	Material	Qty
CHAIR			
A	Back Legs ¾"x¾"x23½"	Clear Pine	2
B	Front Legs ¾"x¾"x18½"	Clear Pine	2
C	Front/Back Stretchers ¾"x¾"x8"	Clear Pine	4
D	Side Stretchers ½"x2½"x9¾"	Clear Pine	1
E	Front/Back Seat Supports ½"x4"x8"	Dowel	1
F	Side Seat Supports ½"x2"x9¾"	Dowel	2
G	Back ½"x2"x8"	Clear Pine	1
H	Arms ½"x2"x10"	Clear Pine	2
I	Footrest ½"x2½"x10¾"	Clear Pine	1

Note: Wood dimensions are listed by thickness, width, and then length.

INSTRUCTIONS

Referring to drawings, *opposite,* and materials chart, *above,* cut all pieces to size. Join pieces with glue and nails, unless noted otherwise.

Drill holes in legs for dowels. Nail together and glue the legs, stretchers, and wood dowels. Clamp and temporarily brace the assembly until the glue sets.

Copy patterns for the chairback and chair arms, *opposite;* transfer to wood and cut. Notch footrest ends to fit around front legs. Attach the back, arms, and footrest with nails and glue. Set nails; fill holes with wood putty. Sand all surfaces; apply varnish or sealer.

Tie the cloth strips to the dowels; weave the seat.

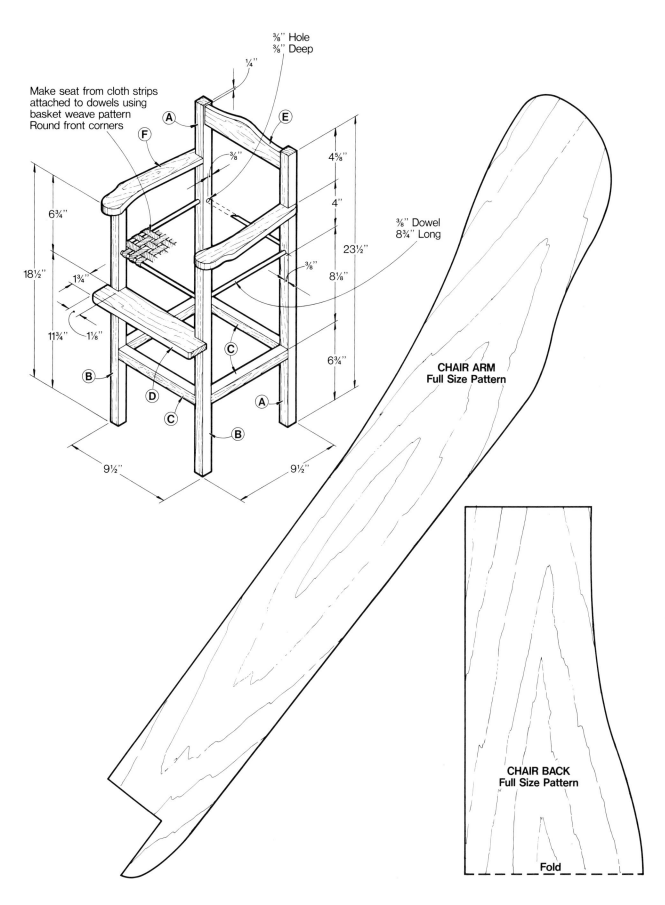

Make seat from cloth strips
attached to dowels using
basket weave pattern
Round front corners

³⁄₈" Hole
³⁄₈" Deep

¼"

Ⓐ

Ⓕ

Ⓔ

³⁄₈"

4⁵⁄₈"

4"

23½"

³⁄₈" Dowel
8¾" Long

³⁄₈"

8¹⁄₈"

6¾"

6¾"

18½"

1¾"

1¹⁄₈"

11¾"

Ⓑ

Ⓓ

Ⓒ

Ⓒ

Ⓐ

Ⓑ

9½"

9½"

CHAIR ARM
Full Size Pattern

CHAIR BACK
Full Size Pattern

Fold

Doll's Wardrobe

Shown on page 36.
Wardrobe is 26x11¼x36 inches.

MATERIALS

Wood as listed in the materials
chart, *right.*
4 wooden drawer pulls with
screws for doors and drawer
Four 1½x1½-inch brass loose-pin
hinges with screws
2 magnetic catches and plates
1¼-inch-long finishing nails
¾-inch-long wire nails
¾-inch-long No. 6 flathead wood
screws
Wood glue; wood putty
Sandpaper; wood stain; varnish

INSTRUCTIONS

Referring to drawing, *opposite,*
cut out pieces. Cut required rabbets,
mortises, holes, dadoes, and other
notches. Assemble pieces with glue
and nails unless noted otherwise.

Using temporary bracing as needed, attach cleat (G) and base sides
(E) to back (C); attach side panels
(A). Fasten base front (F) to base
sides (E) and side panels (A). Install
the bottom (D), shelves (Q), and
apron (H); remove temporary bracing. Glue the block (T) to the center
of the apron (H). Insert wood rod (S)
into the supports (R); fasten supports (R) to the side panels (A) with
glue and screws.

Install top (B). Cut, miter, and attach molding (I) with glue and wire

nails. Assemble doors (N, O, P); install with hinges. Check to make
sure they work; trim excess wood
on door sides to get a good fit. Install
magnetic catches and plates.

Assemble the drawer (J, K, L, M).
Insert it in the bottom opening, making sure it slides in and out easily.

Set nails; fill holes with wood putty. Sand, rounding edges and corners. Stain, varnish, and install door
and drawer pulls.

Child's Clock

Shown on page 36.
Finished clock is 13x8x41 inches.

MATERIALS

Wood as listed in the materials
chart, page 46.
2 wooden door pulls
Four 1½x1½-inch brass loose-pin
hinges with screws
2 magnetic catches and plates
Battery-powered clock motor
Clock hands; Roman numerals
1¼-inch-long finishing nails
¾-inch-long wire nails
Furniture glue; wood putty
Sandpaper; wood stain; varnish

INSTRUCTIONS

Referring to the drawing on page
46, cut all lumber to size. Cut required rabbets, mortises, holes, dadoes, and other notches. Assemble
pieces with glue and nails unless
noted otherwise.

Part	Finished Size	Material	Qty
MATERIALS			
FRAME			
A	Side Panels ½"x10"x35½"	Clear Pine	2
B	Top ½"x11¼"x26"	Clear Pine	1
C	Back ¼"x23½"x35½"	Plywood	1
D	Bottom ½"x10"x23"	Clear Pine	1
E	Base Sides ¾"x1½"x9¼"	Clear Pine	2
F	Base Front ½"x1½"x23"	Clear Pine	1
G	Cleat ½"x¾"x23"	Clear Pine	1
H	Apron ½"x1¼"x23"	Clear Pine	1
I	Cove Molding ⅝"x48"	Pine	1
DRAWER			
J	Front ½"x4⅞"x23"	Clear Pine	1
K	Back ½"x4⅞"x22"	Clear Pine	1
L	Sides ½"x4⅞"x9¾"	Clear Pine	2
M	Bottom ¼"x9¾"x22½"	Hard-board	1
DOORS			
N	Stiles ¾"x2"x11½"	Clear Pine	4
O	Rails ¾"x2"x11½"	Clear Pine	4
P	Panels ½"x8"x12⅛"	Clear Pine	2
INTERIOR			
Q	Shelves ½"x10"x23"	Clear Pine	3
R	Rod Supports ½"x2½"x8"	Clear Pine	2
S	Rod ⅝"x23" or ¾"x23"	Dowel	1
T	Block 1¼"x1½"x7"	Clear Pine	1

Note: Wood dimensions are listed by
thickness, width, and then length.

Using temporary bracing, attach
cleat (G) and base sides (E) to back
(C); attach side panels (A). Fasten
base front (F) to base sides (E) and
side panels (A).

continued

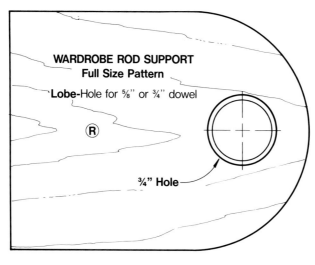

WARDROBE ROD SUPPORT
Full Size Pattern

Lobe-Hole for ⅝" or ¾" dowel

Ⓡ

¾" Hole

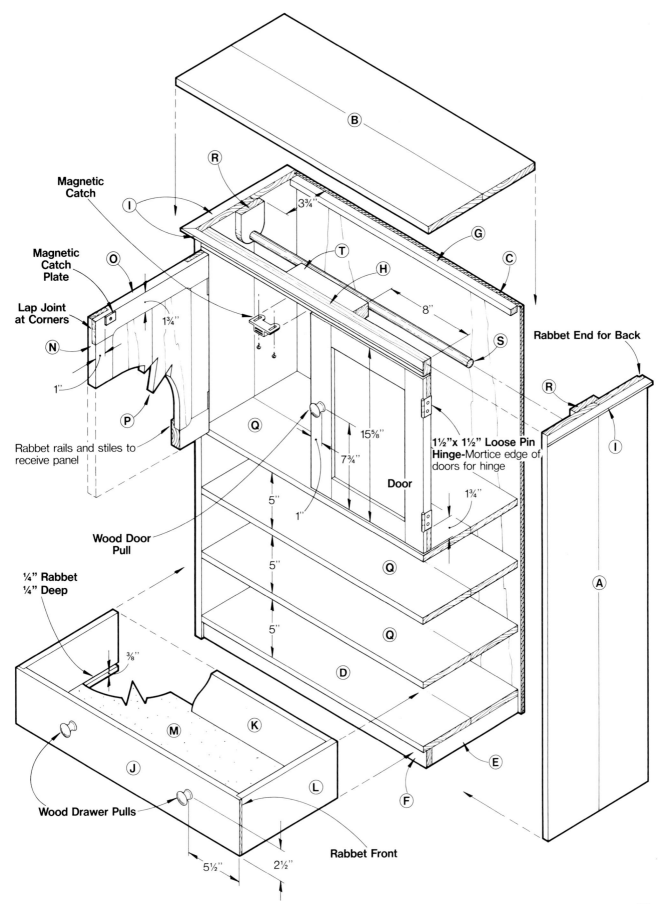

Magnetic Catch

Magnetic Catch Plate

Lap Joint at Corners

3¾"

R

I

B

O

G

T

H

C

1¾"

8"

S

Rabbet rails and stiles to receive panel

1"

N

P

Q

15⅝"

Door

1½"x 1½" Loose Pin Hinge-Mortice edge of doors for hinge

Rabbet End for Back

R

I

7¾"

1¾"

Wood Door Pull

5"

1"

Q

¼" Rabbet ¼" Deep

5"

Q

A

5"

D

⅜"

M

K

E

J

L

F

Wood Drawer Pulls

5½"

2½"

Rabbet Front

45

Install the bottom (D), shelf (P), and apron (H); remove the temporary bracing. Install the top (B). Cut, miter, and attach molding (I) with glue and wire nails.

Cut a circular groove in the clock door panel (L) to define the clockface. Assemble the doors; install them with the hinges. Remove excess wood on the door sides, as needed, to get a good fit. Install the magnetic catches and plates.

Set nails; fill holes. Sand all surfaces, rounding the edges and corners slightly. Stain; install the door pulls, clock motor, and hands. Attach the Roman numerals. Finish with varnish or sealer.

MATERIALS

Part	Finished Size	Material	Qty
FRAME			
A	Side Panels ½″x7″x40½″	Clear Pine	2
B	Top ½″x8″x13″	Clear Pine	1
C	Back ⅛″x10½″x40½″	Hard-board	1
D	Bottom ½″x6⅞″x10″	Clear Pine	1
E	Base Sides ¾″x1½″x6⅛″	Clear Pine	2
F	Base Front ½″x1½″x10″	Clear Pine	1
G	Cleat ¾″x1″x10″	Clear Pine	1
H	Apron ¾″x1¼″x10″	Clear Pine	1
I	Cove Molding ⅝″x36″	Pine	1
CLOCK DOOR			
J	Stiles ¾″x1″x9⅞″	Clear Pine	2
K	Rails ¾″x1″x10″	Clear Pine	2
L	Panel ½″x8½″x8½″	Clear Pine	1
LOWER DOOR			
M	Stiles ¾″x1″x26⅝″	Clear Pine	2
N	Rails ¾″x2″x11½″	Clear Pine	2
O	Panel ½″x8½″x25⅛″	Clear Pine	1
INTERIOR			
P	Shelf ½″x6⅞″x10″	Clear Pine	1

Note: Wood dimensions are listed by thickness, width, and then length.

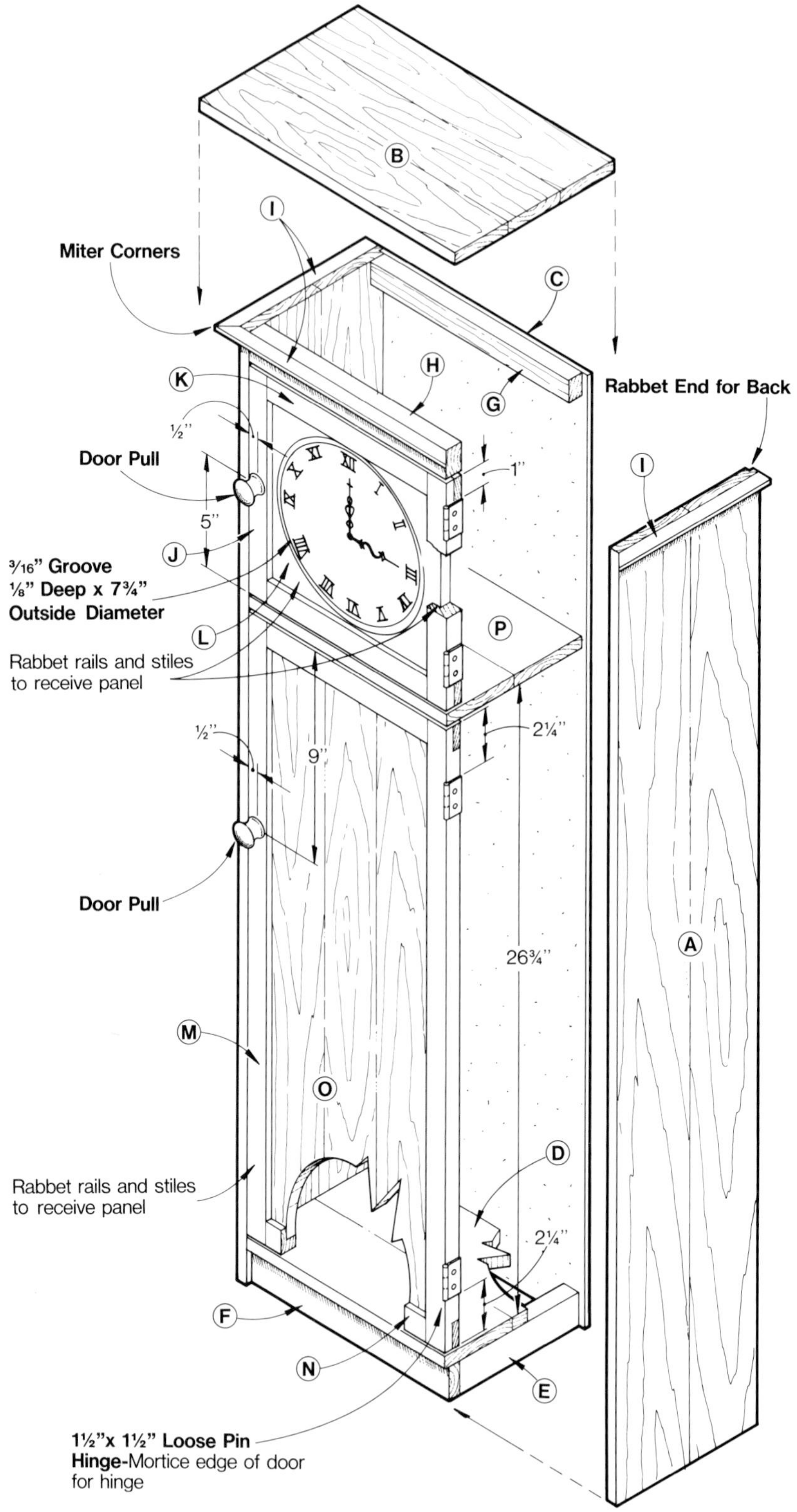
Miter Corners
Rabbet End for Back
Door Pull
½"
1"
5"
3/16" Groove
⅛" Deep x 7¾"
Outside Diameter
Rabbet rails and stiles
to receive panel
½"
9"
2¼"
Door Pull
26¾"
Rabbet rails and stiles
to receive panel
2¼"
1½"x 1½" Loose Pin
Hinge-Mortice edge of door
for hinge
B
I
C
K
H
G
I
J
P
L
A
M
O
D
F
N
E

Quilted-Star
Tree Ornaments

Shown on pages 36–39.
Ornaments are 4½ inches square.

MATERIALS
For each ornament
Scraps of cotton broadcloth fabrics
One 6-inch square of red fabric
One 6-inch square of quilt batting
Cardboard or plastic for templates
Graph paper

INSTRUCTIONS
Make Simple Star and Variable Star ornaments by following the directions below. Measurements are for finished size; add ¼-inch seam allowances when cutting the pieces from fabric.

For the Simple Star
To begin, draw shapes on graph paper and make templates for the patterns as follows: Draw two 2-inch squares. Draw a diagonal line through one square; draw a second diagonal line in the opposite direction to divide the square into four triangles. The square is pattern A; one triangle (a quarter of the square) is pattern B.

Draw two 1-inch squares; divide one square into two triangles. The square is pattern C; one triangle is pattern D.

From fabric scraps cut pieces as follows: one of A, eight of D, and four *each* of C and B. Cut B triangles with the *long* side on fabric grain.

Referring to the piecing diagram, *above right,* sew two D triangles to each B triangle to form rectangles. Stitch rectangles to opposite sides of piece A to make middle row. To make top and bottom rows, sew C squares to ends of remaining rectangles. Sew the three rows together.

Layer a star, batting square, and red backing square. Baste the layers together. Quilt as desired.

Trim the backing to ½ inch larger than the star on all sides. Press in ¼ inch toward the center on all four sides. Bring the folded edges over the raw edges of the star and blindstitch in place, mitering the corners.

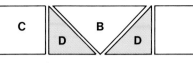
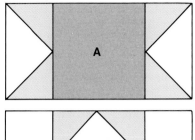
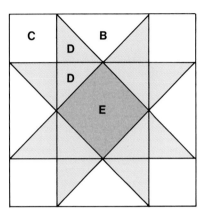

SIMPLE STAR

VARIABLE STAR

Make thread loops to hang the ornaments on the tree or fasten them to the branches with clothespins.

For the Variable Star
Use templates B, C, and D for the Simple Star. On graph paper, draw a 2-inch square. Mark the middle of each side. Draw lines connecting the midpoints, producing a center square (pattern for template E) and four triangles. Make a template for E from cardboard or plastic.

From fabric scraps, cut 1 of piece E, 12 of piece D, and 4 *each* of pieces C and B. Cut B triangles with the *long* side on fabric grain.

To piece the star, sew a D triangle to each side of the E square to make a larger square. To finish piecing the star and to complete the ornament, follow the instructions above for the Simple Star.

Amish Doll Quilts
And Pot Holders

The doll quilts and pot holders are shown on pages 35–37 and 39. The Amish-style doll quilt is 26½x30 inches; the pot holder is 8½x10 inches. The Amish Bars, Center Square, and Center Diamond doll quilts are approximately 26 inches square; the pot holders are approximately 8 inches square.

MATERIALS
For each doll quilt
1 yard of fabric for the quilt back
¼- to ¾-yard pieces of assorted
   fabrics for piecing
32-inch square of quilt batting
4 yards of bias quilt binding

For each pot holder
11-inch square *each* of backing
   fabric and quilt batting
Scraps of assorted fabrics for
   piecing
1¼ yards of bias tape

INSTRUCTIONS
Cutting measurements include ¼-inch seam allowances. Sew pieces with *right* sides facing unless directed otherwise; press seams toward the darker fabric whenever possible. When cutting and piecing each project, refer to the diagrams on pages 48–49. Instructions are for the doll quilts; changes for the pot holders follow in parentheses.

AMISH-STYLE QUILT: Use two fabrics for the Amish-style design. From the first fabric, cut one A piece, 11½x15 (4½x6) inches. Cut two *each* of the following: piece D, 1¾x17½ (¾x6½) inches; piece E, 1¾x16½ (¾x5½) inches; piece H, 4½x22½ (1½x7½) inches; and piece I, 4½x27 (1½x8) inches. From second fabric, cut two *each* of the
continued

following: piece B, 1¾x15 (¾x6) inches; piece C, 1¾x14 (¾x5) inches; piece F, 1¾x20 (¾x7) inches; and piece G, 1¾x19 (¾x6) inches.

Sew the B strips to the long sides of the A rectangle. Sew the C strips to the top and bottom. Repeat for the remaining pieces, adding the strips in alphabetical order to the sides and then to the top and bottom. The quilt top, including ¼-inch seam allowances, should measure approximately 27x30½ (8x9½) inches.

Cut the quilt back and batting 2 inches larger than the quilt top on all sides. Layer and baste the quilt top, batting, and back. Quilt as desired. When quilting is complete, trim the batting and back even with the top. Bind the outer edges with bias tape.

AMISH BARS: Use three fabrics for the Amish Bars design. From the first fabric, cut three A strips, *each* 3½x15½ (1½x5½) inches. From the second fabric, cut two A strips, *each* 3½x15½ (1½x5½) inches. Also, cut four of C, *each* 6½ (2) inches square.

From the third fabric, cut four B strips, *each* 6½x15½ (2x5½) inches.

Alternating colors, sew the five A strips together to make the center. Sew B strips to opposite sides. Add C squares to the ends of the remaining B strips; sew to the remaining sides of the quilt. The quilt top, including seam allowances, should measure approximately 27½ (8½) inches square.

Follow quilting and finishing instructions for the Amish-style quilt, above, to complete the quilt.

CENTER SQUARE: Use three fabrics for the Center Square design. From the first fabric, cut one A piece 10 (4½) inches square.

From the second fabric, cut two B strips, 2½x10 (1x4½) inches, and two C strips, 2½x14 (1x5½) inches. From the third fabric, cut two D strips, 6½x14 (2x5½) inches, and two E strips, 6½x26 (2x8½) inches.

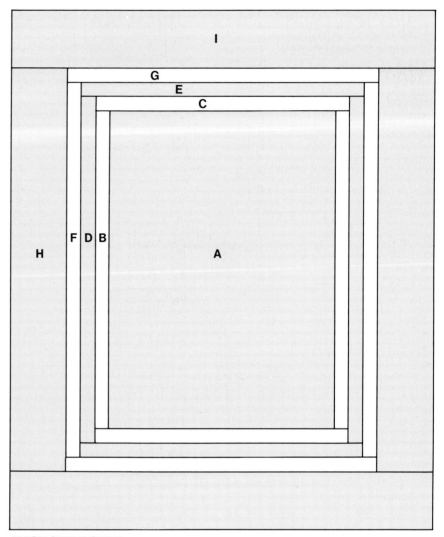

AMISH-STYLE QUILT

Sew the B strips to opposite sides of the center square A. Sew the C strips to the remaining sides. Sew the D strips to opposite sides of the quilt. Sew the E strips to the remaining two sides. The completed quilt top should measure approximately 26 (8½) inches square, including seam allowances.

Follow quilting and finishing instructions for the Amish-style quilt, above, to complete the quilt.

CENTER DIAMOND: Use three fabrics for the Center Diamond design. From the first fabric, cut one A piece, 5½ (2½) inches square. For the D triangles, cut two squares, *each* 6 (3) inches square. Cut each square in half diagonally to make two triangles (four total).

From the second fabric, cut two *each* of the following: strip B, 1½x5½ (⅞x2½) inches; strip C, 1½x7½ (⅞x3¼) inches; strip E, 2½x10½ (1x4½) inches; and strip F, 2½x14½ (1x5½) inches. From the third fabric, cut two G strips, *each* 6½x14½ (2x5½) inches, and two H strips, *each* 6½x26½ (2x8½) inches.

Sew the B strips to opposite sides of the A square. Add the C strips to the remaining sides. Sew the *long*

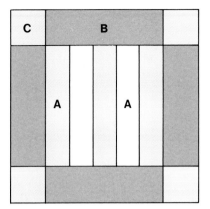

AMISH BARS

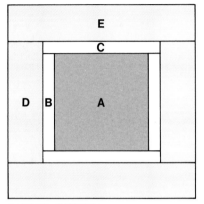

CENTER SQUARE

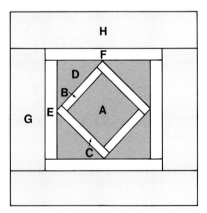

CENTER DIAMOND

sides of two D triangles to opposite sides of the center; repeat for the remaining two D triangles.

Sew E strips to opposite sides of quilt top; repeat for F, G, and H strips. The quilt top should measure approximately 26½ (8½) inches square, including seam allowances.

Follow quilting and finishing instructions for the Amish-style quilt, page 48, to complete the quilt.

Country Doll

Shown on pages 37 and 38.
Finished doll is 24 inches tall.

MATERIALS

½ yard of muslin for face and body
½ yard of white cotton for legs, panties, and bonnet
Black felt for boots
Six ¼-inch-diameter beads or buttons for boots
Embroidery floss in the following colors: tan, blue, white, pink, and black
Polyester fiberfill; yarn for hair
½ yard *each* of coordinating fabrics for dress and pinafore
1 yard *each* of ¼-inch-wide elastic and ribbon
½ yard of ½-inch-wide lace for bonnet
Four ½-inch-diameter buttons for pinafore
Powdered rouge; dressmaker's carbon

INSTRUCTIONS

Trace the doll patterns on pages 50–52; enlarge clothing patterns on page 53. The patterns include ¼-inch seam allowances, except for the shoe pattern, which includes a ⅛-inch seam allowance. Sew pieces with *right* sides facing unless directed otherwise.

To make the doll

From muslin, cut one *each* of the face, body front, and chin. Cut two body backs and four arms. From white fabric, cut four legs.

Transfer the face pattern to the right side of the face fabric, using dressmaker's carbon. Embroider the features onto the face using three strands of embroidery floss.

Stitch the dart in the body front. Sew arm sections together, leaving an opening in the *side* for stuffing. Do not stitch across arm tops. Turn right side out. Baste arms to body front (they will be stuffed later).

Sew the long edge of the chin, opposite the neck edge, to the lower edge of the face. Stitch the neck edge of the chin to the body front at the neckline.

Sew the center back seam. Sew the body back to the front and face, stitching across the arms and leaving the lower end open for stuffing. Turn right side out.

Sew the leg sections together, leaving an opening in the *side* for stuffing. Do not stitch across the leg tops. Turn right side out. Stitch the legs to the body front (they will be stuffed later).

Firmly stuff the body and head. Turn under the raw edges of the lower body back; slip-stitch closed. Stuff the arms and the legs; slip-stitch closed.

Hand-sew yarn to the head, making loops over finger for curls.

To make the clothing

DRESS: From dress fabric, cut one *each* of skirt front, bodice/sleeve front, and neck binding and tie. Cut two *each* of the skirt back, bodice/sleeve back, and collar.

Gather top edge of the skirt front and back pieces. Sew skirt front to bodice/sleeve front; repeat for back pieces. Starting at the bottom edge, sew up 6 inches of the center back dress seam. Press under the remaining seam allowances (up to the neckline); edge-stitch. Sew the dress front to the back at the shoulders.

Narrowly hem the straight edge of both collars; gather curved edges. Sew collars to neckline, adjusting gathers to fit. Collars will meet at the center front.

Matching centers, sew the right side of the neck binding to the wrong side of the neckline, extending the tie ends. Press in the seam allowances along the tie ends. Fold the binding to the right side, over seam allowances, turning under the raw edges. Sew the open edges of the tie ends and neck binding. Knot the ends of the ties.

Narrowly hem the lower edges of the sleeves and the dress. On the wrong side of each sleeve, center a 5-inch piece of elastic over the line indicated on the pattern. Stitch through the center of the elastic, stretching the elastic as you stitch. Sew the side and underarm seams.

continued

49

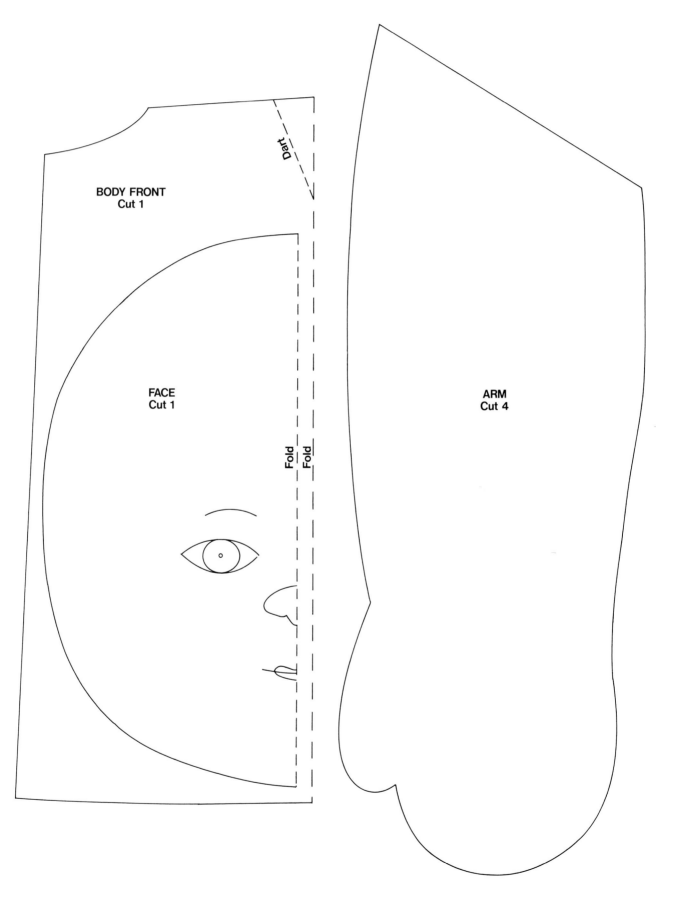

BODY FRONT
Cut 1

Dart

FACE
Cut 1

Fold Fold

ARM
Cut 4

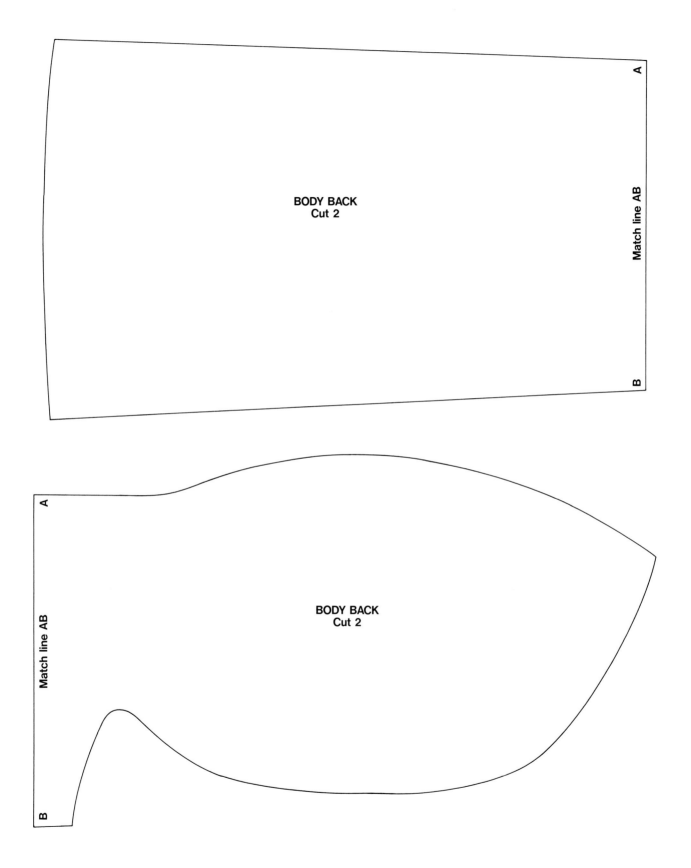

BODY BACK
Cut 2

Match line AB

A

B

Match line AB

BODY BACK
Cut 2

A

B

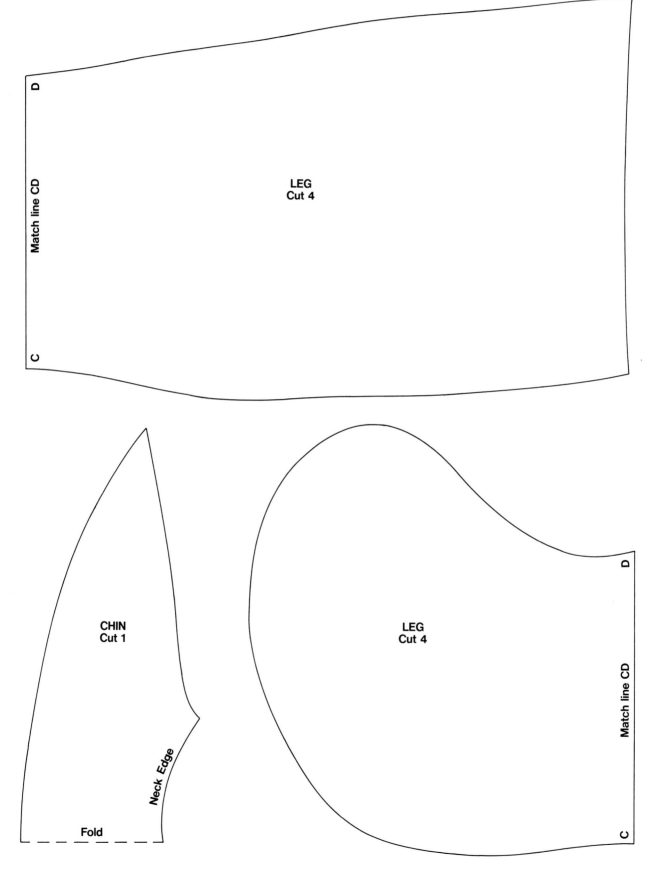

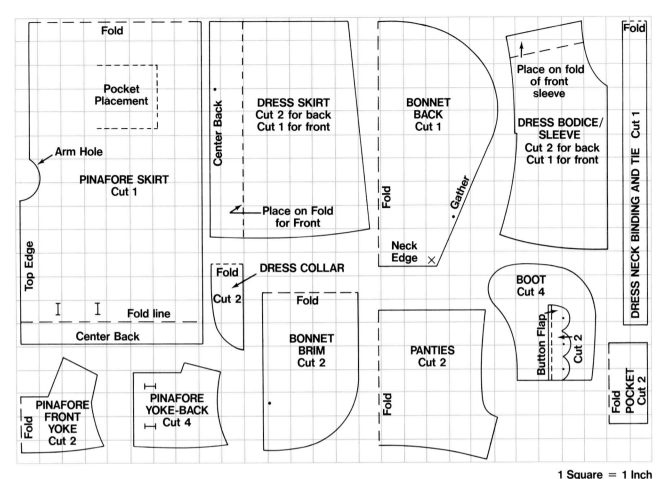

1 Square = 1 Inch

PINAFORE: Cut one pinafore skirt, two front yokes, two pockets, and four back yokes from the pinafore fabric. Fold under ¾ inch along top edge of pocket; hem. Turn under ¼ inch on the side and bottom edges of the pockets and press. Sew the pockets to the pinafore skirt.

Press, then stitch under ¼ inch along curved armholes of the skirt, clipping as necessary. Press the skirt extensions to the wrong side, forming facings. Narrowly hem the lower skirt edge. Sew a gathering thread along the top skirt edge.

Stitch the yoke front to the yoke back at the shoulder seams; repeat for the yoke lining. Press under ¼ inch on the lower edges of the yoke lining. Sew yoke to yoke lining along the back, neck, and armhole edges. Clip and turn right side out.

Sew the skirt to the yoke, gathering the skirt to fit. Press the seam toward the yoke; slip-stitch the lining over the seam. Make buttonholes on the left back; sew buttons on the right back.

PANTIES: From the white fabric, cut two panties. Sew the center front seam. Turn under ½ inch on the leg and waist openings to form casings; sew in place. Insert 12 inches of elastic into the waistline casing and 3 inches into each leg casing. Sew the center back seam, catching the ends of the elastic in the stitching. Sew the crotch seam, catching the ends of the elastic.

BOOTS: Cut four boots and two boot button flaps from the black felt. Use ⅛-inch seams for the boots. Topstitch a button flap onto the outer boot pieces, as indicated on pattern. Sew black buttons or beads at the dots, stitching through all layers.

Sew the inner boot pieces to the outer boot pieces. Edge-stitch the upper edges of the boots.

BONNET: From white fabric, cut one bonnet back and two bonnet brims. Narrowly hem the neck edge of the bonnet back. Gather the remaining edge between the dots.

Join the curved edges of the brim. Clip seam; turn and press. Gather the bonnet onto one brim piece, matching the dots; keep the other piece free. Press under ¼ inch on the remaining brim edge. Slip-stitch the folded edge over the gathering, encasing the raw edges.

Topstitch lace to the brim edge, turning under the raw edges of the lace ends. To form the bonnet ties, cut the ribbon in half. Loop one end of each ribbon piece and tack in place at the position indicated by an X on the bonnet pattern.

Barnyard Friends

Rural kids (and city kids, too!) will have hours of fun playing with these farm animals. For toddlers there's a riding horse, and for children—or grown-ups—there are familiar barnyard favorites full of folk-art charm. Make just one or a herd or a flock to win the heart of a child.

A dappled mare, pig family, and push-and-pull-along ram and cow are projects for the woodworker in your family. The sculptured look is created by gluing together different shapes and rounding the edges with a sander. Rope tails and simple painting add realism with a touch of whimsy.

Construct a wooden riding horse, *opposite, above,* using simple shapes and techniques. The front is hinged for easy steering and provides many hours of galloping fun for toddlers.

Pig Family

Shown on pages 54 and 55.
Sow is 17 inches long; piglets are
11 inches long.

MATERIALS

For all pigs
Scraps of ⅜-inch-diameter
   clothesline for tails
Finishing nails
Wood glue
Wood clamps; rasp
Drill; ⅛-inch and ⅜-inch bits
Pink, black, and gray acrylic paints
Paintbrush
Artist's paintbrushes

For one sow
Three 1x10-inch pine boards, *each*
   18 inches long, for the center
   body and left and right center
   body sections
Two 1x10-inch pine boards, *each*
   14 inches long, for the body
   sides
⅛-inch-diameter wooden dowel

For one piglet
Three 1x8-inch pine boards, *each*
   12 inches long

INSTRUCTIONS

Enlarge the master patterns for
the piglet, *right,* and sow, *opposite.*

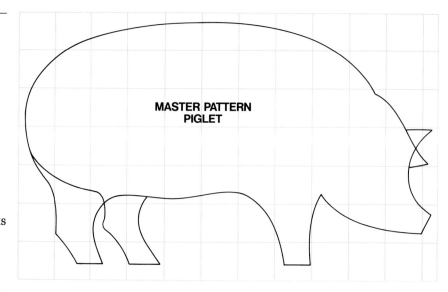

MASTER PATTERN
PIGLET

1 Square = 1 Inch

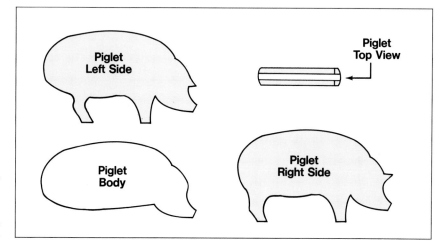

**Piglet
Left Side**

**Piglet
Top View**

**Piglet
Body**

**Piglet
Right Side**

FOR THE SOW: Referring to the assembly diagrams for the sow (below
the master pattern), trace appropriate lines to make patterns for the
center body, right center body, left
center body, right side, and left side.

Craft the sow from five layers of
wood. Transfer each of the five sow
patterns onto appropriate boards.
Cut one of each piece using a band
saw or coping saw.

Glue and clamp the three center
body pieces together; let dry completely. Cut out the center of the inner layers to reduce weight, leaving
a 1-inch margin around the edges.
Attach body sides with nails and
glue. Clamp pieces together until
dry. Using a rasp, round all of the
edges slightly; sand until smooth.

Drill six ⅛-inch-diameter holes in
the sow's udder for her nipples. Cut
six ½-inch-long pieces of dowel for
the nipples. Attach the dowel pieces
in the holes with glue.

Drill a ⅜-inch-diameter hole for
the tail. Cut a short piece of clothesline for the tail. Insert the clothesline
in the hole and glue in place.

Paint the sow pink; let dry and
sand lightly. Paint the sow with a
second coat of pink paint. Using artist's paintbrushes, paint black and
gray spots as desired (see photograph for ideas).

FOR EACH PIGLET: Referring to
the assembly diagrams for the piglet
(below the master pattern), trace the
appropriate lines to make patterns
for the body, right side, and left side.

Craft piglets from three layers of
wood. To make one piglet, trace the
patterns onto boards. Using a band
saw or coping saw, cut one body,
one right side, and one left side.

Glue the three pieces together.
Clamp until dry. Using a rasp, round
all of the edges slightly. Sand the
edges and piglet body until smooth.

Paint with two coats of pink paint,
sanding lightly between coats. Paint
black and gray spots as desired (see
photograph for ideas).

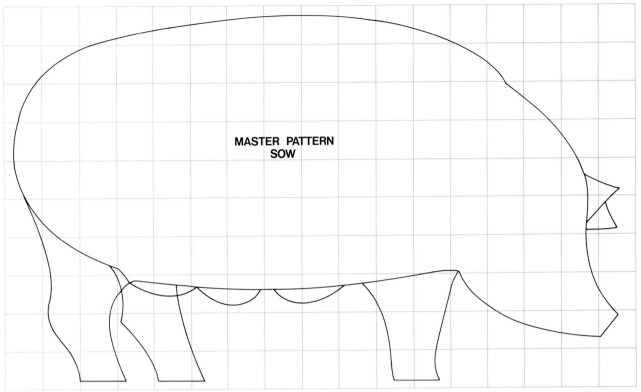

MASTER PATTERN
SOW

1 Square = 1 Inch

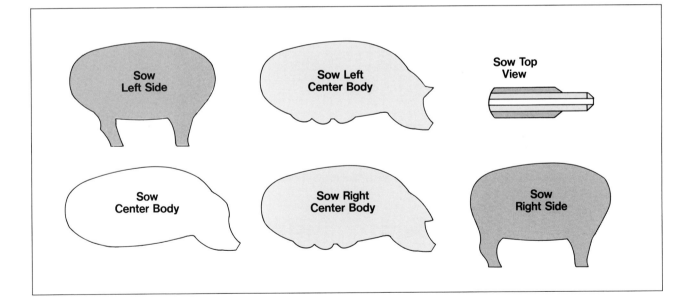

Sow
Left Side

Sow Left
Center Body

Sow Top
View

Sow
Center Body

Sow Right
Center Body

Sow
Right Side

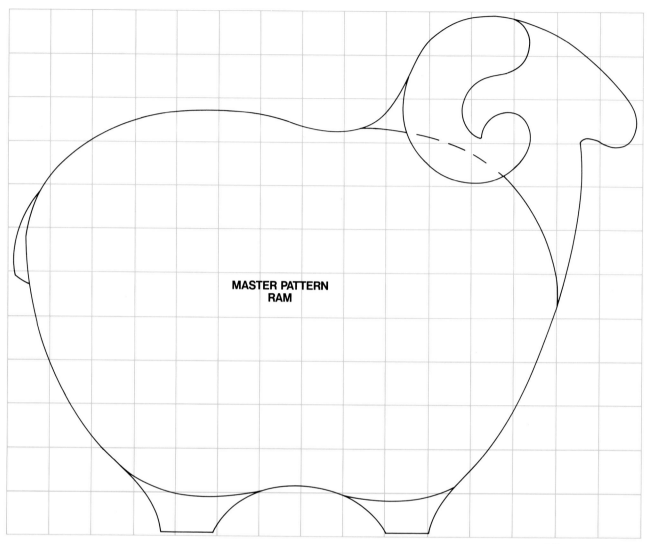

**MASTER PATTERN
RAM**

1 Square = 1 Inch

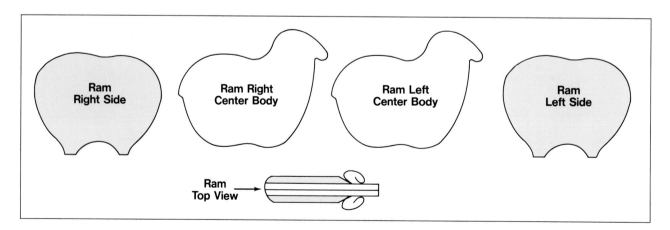

Ram
Right Side

Ram Right
Center Body

Ram Left
Center Body

Ram
Left Side

Ram
Top View

Push-Along Ram

Shown on page 55.
Finished ram is 15 inches long.

MATERIALS

Two 1x12x16-inch pine boards for
the right and left body centers
Two 1x12x13-inch pine boards for
the body sides
1x8x15-inch pine board for base
Two 1x1x7½-inch pine boards for
the axle casings
Two ¼-inch-diameter dowels,
each 9 inches long, for the axles
Drill; ¼-inch bit
Four washers; wood glue
Finishing nails; screws
White, tan, black, brown, purple,
green, and blue-green acrylic
paints
Paintbrush; artist's paintbrush

INSTRUCTIONS

Enlarge the master pattern for the
ram, *opposite.*

Referring to the assembly diagrams below the master pattern,
trace the appropriate lines to make
the patterns for the right body center, left body center, right side, left
side, and horns.

Make the ram from four layers of
wood. Transfer each of the ram
body patterns onto the appropriate
boards. Cut one of each piece using
a band saw or coping saw.

Cut the center out of body center
pieces to reduce weight, leaving a 1-
inch margin. Glue and clamp together the center bodies; let dry.

Attach the body sides with nails
and glue. Clamp the pieces together
until dry. Round all of the edges
slightly and sand until smooth.

Paint the ram with two coats of
white paint, sanding lightly between
coats. Referring to the photograph
on page 55, add details with tan
paint as desired. Paint the ram's
head black.

Cut two horns from scrap wood;
round, then sand the edges. Angle
the top side of the horns to fit the
head. Paint the horns with two coats
of brown paint, sanding lightly between the coats. With an artist's
paintbrush, add stripe details with
black paint; let dry. Glue and nail
the horns in place; clamp until dry.

To construct the base, cut or dado
a trough into each axle casing to accept a ¼-inch-diameter dowel. Glue
and nail the axle casings to the
base, 2 inches in from the ends.

From wood scraps, cut four 3-
inch-diameter circles for the wheels.
Drill a ¼-inch-diameter hole in the
center of each wheel to accept the
dowel axles.

Referring to the photograph on
page 55, paint the wheels and the
base. Slip washers on the axles as
spacers. Glue on the wheels.

Attach the ram to the base with
wood screws.

Dapple-Gray Horse

Shown on page 55.
*Finished horse is approximately 17
inches tall.*

MATERIALS

Two 1x12x19-inch pine boards for
right and left center body pieces
Four 1x8x14-inch pine boards for
the left and right body sides
Drill; ⅜-inch and ½-inch bits
2 yards of Manila rope
Scrap of gray felt for ears
Wood glue; finishing nails
Black, white, and pink acrylic
paints
Small sponge (for painting)
Paintbrush; artist's paintbrush

INSTRUCTIONS

Enlarge the master pattern for the
horse, page 60. Referring to the assembly diagrams below the master
pattern, trace the appropriate lines
to make the patterns for the right
body center, left body center, left
side, right side, and ear.

Craft the horse from four layers of
wood. Transfer the center body patterns to the 1x12-inch boards. Cut
out the center body pieces using a
band saw or coping saw.

Glue and clamp the two center
body pieces together; let dry completely. Cut the middle out of the
center body to reduce weight, leaving a 1-inch margin.

For the left side, transfer left side
pattern for horse to two 1x8x14-inch
boards lying side by side with grain
running vertically. Cut out left side
pieces. Repeat for right side.

Attach the body sides to the body
center with nails and glue; clamp together until dry. Round the edges
lightly using a rasp, and sand the
horse lightly.

For the mane, drill a ⅜-inch hole
between the ear position marks and
eight holes along the neck. Cut 4-
inch lengths of rope; glue rope in the
holes for the mane.

Drill a ½-inch-diameter hole for
the tail. Cut two 10-inch lengths of
rope; glue in the hole. Unravel the
rope mane and tail.

Mix several shades of gray paint.
Paint horse the lightest shade; let
dry. Sponge on darker paint shades
for a dappled effect, letting each col-
or dry before adding next color. Add
nose, eye, and hoof details.

Cut two ears from gray felt. Pleat
the bottom of each ear; glue or staple the ears to the horse's head at
the positioning marks.

Pull-Along Cow

Shown on page 54.
Finished cow is 16½ inches long.

MATERIALS

2x12x19-inch pine board for the
body center
Two 1x12x14-inch pine boards for
the left and right body sides
1x8x15-inch pine board for base
Two 1x1x7½-inch pine boards for
the axle casings
¼-inch-diameter wood dowel
½-inch-diameter wood dowel
Drill; ¼-inch and ½-inch bits
Wood glue; wood rasp
11 inches of Manila rope
Four washers; screw eye
Scraps of black felt for ears
Four screws; finishing nails
Colored cord; 1-inch-diameter
wooden bead
Black, white, blue-green, purple,
brown, and pink acrylic paints
Paintbrush; artist's paintbrush
continued

59

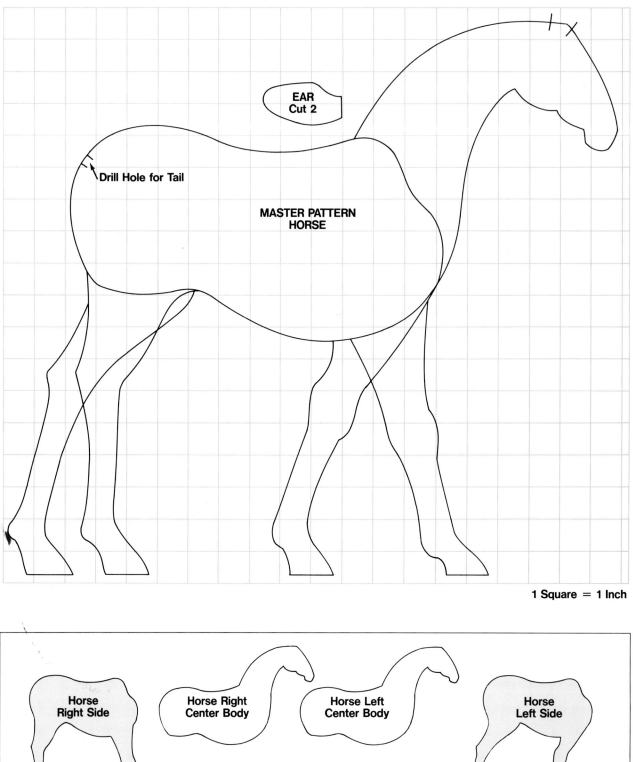

EAR
Cut 2

Drill Hole for Tail

MASTER PATTERN
HORSE

1 Square = 1 Inch

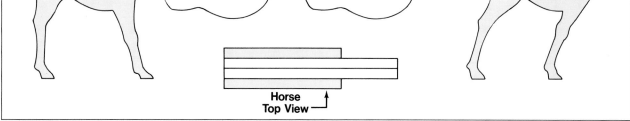

Horse
Right Side

Horse Right
Center Body

Horse Left
Center Body

Horse
Left Side

Horse
Top View

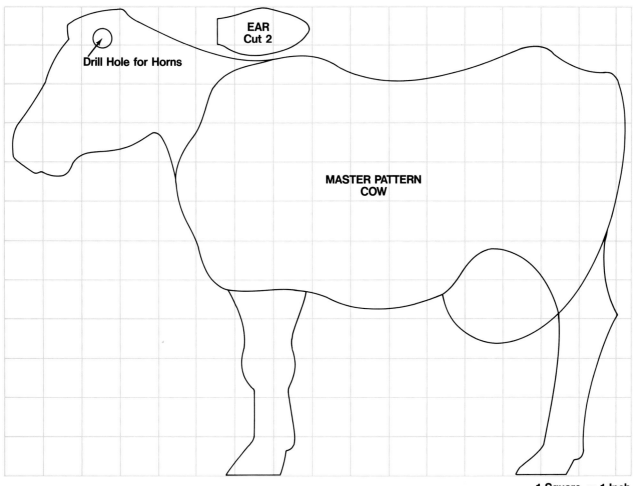

Drill Hole for Horns

EAR
Cut 2

MASTER PATTERN
COW

1 Square = 1 Inch

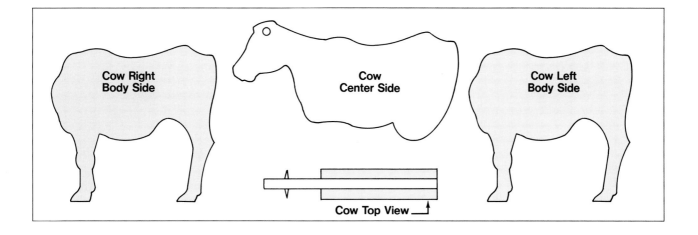

Cow Right
Body Side

Cow
Center Side

Cow Left
Body Side

Cow Top View

INSTRUCTIONS

Enlarge the master pattern for the cow, page 61.

Referring to the assembly diagram beneath the master pattern, trace the appropriate lines to make patterns for the center body, right side, left side, and ear.

Make the cow from three layers of wood. Transfer the cow center body pattern to the 2x12-inch board and the body side patterns to the 1x12-inch boards. Cut out the body pieces. Cut the middle out of the center body to reduce weight, leaving a 1-inch margin.

Glue the body sides to the center body; clamp and allow to dry. Sand lightly, rounding all of the edges.

Drill four ¼-inch-diameter holes in the udder for the teats. Cut four 1½-inch-long dowels. With a rasp, round the dowel ends; glue dowels into holes in the udder.

For horns, cut a 4-inch-long piece from a ½-inch-diameter dowel. Using a rasp, file the ends of the dowel to form smooth and tapered ends. Sand the dowel; paint it black.

At the position indicated on the pattern for the horns, drill a ½-inch-diameter hole through the cow's head. Drill a ¼-inch-diameter hole for the tail.

Paint the cow with two coats of white paint, sanding lightly between coats. Paint nose and udder pink. Paint hooves black; paint black spots on the cow as desired (see photograph). Paint the eyes brown, adding white highlights, if desired.

For the tail, glue rope in the hole and partially unravel the end to make a tuft.

Slide the tapered dowel through hole in the cow's head; glue in place.

Cut two ears from black felt. Form a pleat at the bottom of the ears and staple or glue them to the head.

For the base, cut out or dado a trough into the axle casings to fit ¼-inch-diameter dowels. Glue and nail the axle casings to the base, 2 inches in from the ends. Paint the base blue-green.

Cut four 3-inch-diameter circles from 1-inch-thick wood scraps for the wheels. Drill a ¼-inch-diameter hole in the center of each wheel to receive the dowel axle. Paint the wheels purple.

Cut two 9-inch-long axles from the ¼-inch-diameter dowel. Insert the dowels into the axle casings. Add washers as spacers. Glue on the wheels.

Attach the screw eye at the center front of the base. Tie one end of the pull cord to the screw eye. Slip the bead on the other cord end; knot the cord to hold the bead in place.

Riding Horse

Shown on page 55.
Finished horse is 22 inches tall.

MATERIALS

1⅛x11x24-inch pine board for the body
1⅛x9x23-inch pine board for head
Two 1⅛x5x8-inch pine boards for the saddle
Four 1x8x8-inch pine boards for the wheels
¾-inch-diameter wooden dowel, 7½ inches long, for handle
Two 1⅛-inch-diameter wooden dowels, each 3¾ inches long
¼-inch steel axle stock and axle sleeve assembly
Eight ¼-inch washers
Four hammer-on axle caps
3½-inch butt hinge
Six ⅞-inch-long countersink wood screws
Finishing nails
Wood glue
Wood filler
Sandpaper
Varnish

INSTRUCTIONS

Enlarge patterns, *opposite,* onto paper. Noting the wood grain indications, transfer the patterns to the boards. Cut out the wood pieces. Sand all pieces to round the corners and smooth the edges.

Taper the fronts of the saddle pieces to ½ inch thick. Glue and nail the saddle to the body piece.

Using a drill, bore a ¾-inch-diameter hole through the horse's neck for the handle. Insert the handle dowel; anchor the handle with a nail going through neck into dowel.

Cut slots in the body and head pieces to fit the hinge, referring to the pattern for the location. To allow the head and body to pivot, round corners to a ½-inch radius where the body and the head meet.

Insert the hinge into the body slot. Using a drill bit just large enough in diameter to accommodate the screw shaft, drill three holes through one side of the wood into the hinge leaf, missing the predrilled holes. Drill through the hinge but not through the wood on the other side.

Install the screws flush with the wood surface. Apply wood filler to any visible part of the slot.

Insert the remaining half of the hinge into the head slot. Repeat the drilling and installation instructions to attach the hinge in the head.

For the rear axle assembly, drill a hole through the leg and *lengthwise* through each 1⅛x3¾-inch dowel. Drill the holes just large enough to accommodate the axle sleeve assembly with a snug fit.

Cut a steel axle 10¾ inches long and an axle sleeve 8⅝ inches long. Slip the axle sleeve through one dowel, through horse, and through the second dowel. Insert the steel axle in the sleeve.

For the front axle assembly, drill a hole through the horse just large enough for the axle sleeve assembly to fit snugly. Cut the steel axle 3¼ inches long and the axle sleeve 1⅛ inches long. Insert the axle sleeve and axle into the hole.

To attach the wheels, slip a washer on the axle. Drill a ¼-inch-diameter hole in the wheel center. Then, slide on the wheel and a second washer. Hammer on the wheel cap. Repeat for the other wheels.

Sand all parts until smooth. Finish the horse with two coats of polyurethane varnish, sanding lightly between coats.

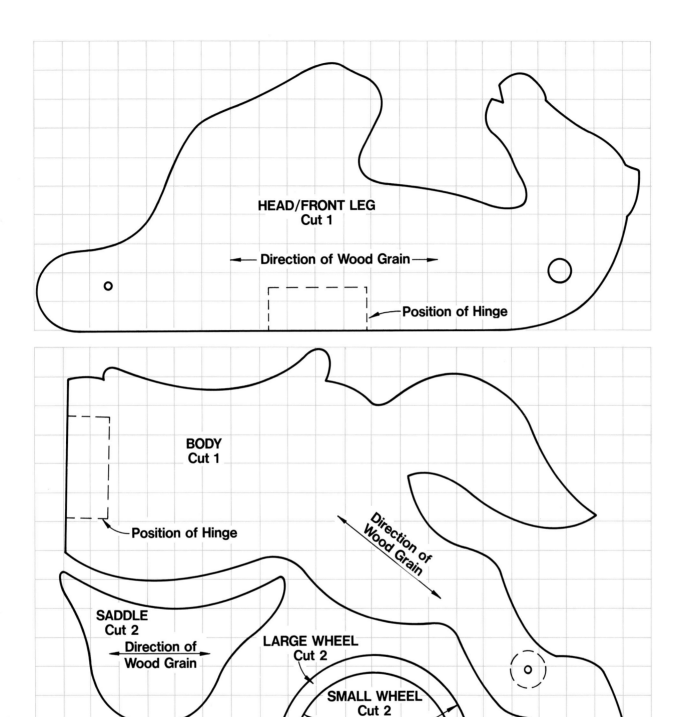

HEAD/FRONT LEG
Cut 1

◄— Direction of Wood Grain —►

Position of Hinge

BODY
Cut 1

Position of Hinge

Direction of
Wood Grain

SADDLE
Cut 2

Direction of
Wood Grain

LARGE WHEEL
Cut 2

SMALL WHEEL
Cut 2

R = 3"   R = 3½"

Fold

1 Square = 1 Inch

Woodland Holiday

Winter without and warmth within—and an inviting blend of ruggedness and grace—make this woodland Christmas merry. Whimsical twig trims, traditional Indian rugs, bead-bedecked Victorian accents, even a lacy skirt for the tree, live together joyously in this rustic cabin dressed for the season. For a high-spirited holiday, try a similar mix of styles, textures, and crafting techniques in your own home.

Twig chairs, diminutive copies of their grown-up cousins, are easy to make from willow or alder saplings (or clippings from your own backyard). For stars, wire together 6-inch-long twigs or vines and paint them, if you wish.

Beaded stars hang on the tree, *right*. Sew them from scraps of velveteen in deep colors.

Directions for the projects in this chapter begin on page 70.

Part of the pleasure of crafting with natural materials is in gathering them for your projects. An afternoon's walk in the woods may be all you need to find the tawny autumn leaves and lichens and the twigs and branches for the designs shown here. If you don't have access to the recommended materials, let your imagination guide you to attractive substitutes.

An oversize, lavishly fringed stocking makes an elegant gift wrap for a special bottle of New Year's champagne and some exquisite crystal goblets. The cuff on this 22½-inch wool stocking is embellished with a woodland floral needlepoint motif and beaded fringe.

Use twigs and bark to craft the 22x27-inch frame, *above,* and birch branches for the candlesticks.

A beaded velvet star lends softness to a woodland wreath of moss and bark. The wreath is easily made by gluing natural materials to a straw base.

Beautiful beading highlights this hand-knit woodland sweater, *right*. For experienced stitchers, the design is worked on circular needles, with beads knitted directly into the snowflakelike patterns on the yoke, sleeve, and lower body. If you're not ready to tackle such a challenging project, you can achieve a similar effect by adding beads to a purchased pullover.

Scraps of velveteen, fleece, and embroidered trims are the primary materials for the Eskimo family, *opposite*. The appealing expressions on these 11- and 14-inch dolls are sure to please every doll lover.

For crafters, one of the delights of cold weather (or cooler temperatures in temperate zones) is working with the hefty yarns and fabrics set aside during warmer months. When the air turns chilly, you'll enjoy stitching with the wool, velveteen, fur, and other materials used for these projects as much as you'll delight in the pleasure such special gifts bring to your loved ones.

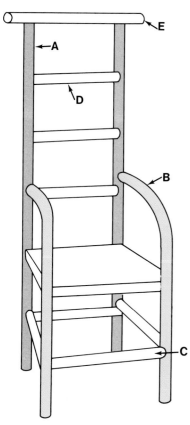

LADDER-BACK CHAIR

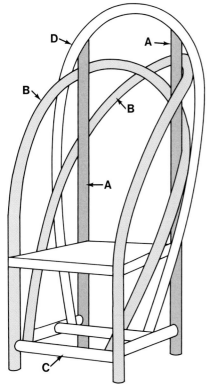

WRAP AROUND-ARM CHAIR

Miniature Twig Chairs

Shown on page 64.
Finished chairs are approximately 10 inches tall.

MATERIALS
Pliable shoots from trees such as
    willow or alder
Pruning shears
Small handsaw
Ruler or tape measure
Finishing nails
Cedar shingles or wood scraps
    for seats
Rubber bands

INSTRUCTIONS
Use pruning shears to cut an assortment of twigs, collecting more than you will need. *Note:* To keep twigs supple, stand them in a bucket of warm water until you're ready to use them.

FOR THE LADDER-BACK CHAIR: Cut twigs in the following numbers and sizes: two twigs 10 to 11 inches long for the back legs (A), two twigs 10 to 11 inches long for the front legs and arms (B), four twigs 4 inches long for the bottom braces (C), three twigs 4 inches long for the ladder-backs (D), and one twig 6 inches long for the top rail (E).

Cut a 4½-inch square from a cedar shingle or from scrap wood for each chair seat. Cut ¼-inch notches at each corner for the chair legs.

Following the diagram, *left,* nail the back legs (A) to the seat at the back corner-cutouts.

Nail front legs (B) to front corner-cutouts. Leave arm extensions free until braces are attached.

Fit the braces (C) between the legs and nail them in place. *Slowly and carefully* bend the arms and nail them to the chairback. Add the ladder-backs (D), nailing them from the outside of the back legs. Lay the top rail (E) in place and nail to the top of the back legs.

Wrap rubber bands around the bottom of the legs to secure chair until wood dries (five to 10 days).

FOR THE WRAPAROUND ARM-CHAIR: Cut twigs in the following numbers and sizes: two twigs 10 inches long for back legs (A), two twigs 20 to 22 inches long for front legs and arm wraps (B), four twigs 4 inches long for bottom braces (C), and one twig 22 inches long for the top rail (D).

Cut the seat the same as for the ladder-back chair.

Following the diagram, *left,* nail the back legs (A) to the seat at the back corner-cutouts.

Nail front legs (B) to front corner-cutouts, leaving arm-wrap portion free. Nail the braces (C) in place.

Slowly and gently, bend each arm wrap (B) up and around both back legs (A). Secure each arm to the seat side with nails.

Place the top arched rail (D) inside the bottom side braces (C). Wrap the rail over the *top* of the back legs (A). Nail the arched rail (D) to back legs (A) and arms (B).

Wrap rubber bands around the bottom of the legs to secure chair until wood dries (five to 10 days).

Twig Star Ornaments
Shown on pages 64 and 65.
Finished stars are approximately 6 inches across.

MATERIALS
5 small twigs about 6 inches long
    for each star
Carpet thread, string, or fine wire
Spray paint in the color of your
    choice (white, silver, or gold)

INSTRUCTIONS
Lay out five twigs to form a star. Using string, thread, or fine wire, bind the twigs together at the ends and at the twig intersections.

Tie a thread loop at one point, to hang the star.

Spray-paint the star if desired.

Twig Picture Frame

Shown on page 67.
Finished frame is approximately 22x27 inches.

MATERIALS

One 12x17-inch picture mat with an 8½x11-inch oval or rectangular opening
One 12x17-inch sheet of bark (see instructions below)
Two 22-inch-long branches, approximately 1 inch in diameter, for the horizontal crossbars
Two 27-inch-long branches, approximately 1 inch in diameter, for the vertical crossbars
Four 50-inch-long willow branches, approximately ½ inch in diameter
Contact cement
Tape measure
Hammer; nails
Staple gun; staples or carpet tacks
Chisel; mallet
Sharp pocketknife
Drill; ⅛-inch bit

INSTRUCTIONS

Note: Use bark from recently fallen trees. Stripping bark from a live tree may cause the tree to die.

TO MAKE BARK MATTING: Peel the bark from a branch by scoring a deep line lengthwise through the bark with a sharp knife. Make two cuts around the log, marking the section of bark to be removed. Place the tip of a chisel along the scored line; gently tap it with a mallet. Continue until the bark is removed.

Press bark pieces between heavy books to keep them flat until you are ready to use them.

Spread the *right* side of the mat and the *wrong* side of the bark sheet with contact cement. Press the bark sheet and mat firmly together to bond them. Cover the project with paper or cloth for protection; weight the layers with heavy books.

When cement is dry, carefully trim bark from the frame opening, using a sharp pocketknife.

TO ASSEMBLE THE FRAME: Place the two horizontal crossbars along the top and bottom of the mat; lay the vertical crossbars atop the horizontal crossbars and along the sides of the mat. Mark the crossbar intersections; notch both the top and bottom branches at each intersection so they will lie flush when they are fitted together.

At each corner, drill a pilot hole for a nail from the back through one crossbar and partially into the second crossbar. Fit the crossbars together and nail the frame corners.

Mount a picture, a photograph, or needlework in the mat. Staple the mat to the frame back, or attach it with carpet tacks.

Next, *gently* bend a willow bough into a loop. Fit the loop around the corner of the frame. Nail bough to frame from the back and to ends of the crossbars from the outside. Repeat, looping and nailing the remaining willow boughs. Nail the willow boughs from the back where they cross each other, as well.

Twig Candlesticks

Shown on pages 65 and 67.
Finished candlesticks range from 2½ to 10 inches tall.

MATERIALS

Birch limbs 1½ to 3 inches in diameter
Saw
Sharp pocketknife
Drill; ¾-inch auger bit
Candles

INSTRUCTIONS

Using a saw, cut the birch limbs into pieces 2½ to 10 inches long. The tops and bottoms of the pieces should be flat so candlesticks will stand straight.

To make scallop-top candlesticks, carve arcs into the top rim of each candlestick.

For a simply finished top on your candlestick, carve a fine line around the rim of the branch to remove the top layer of rough bark and expose the smooth inner bark.

In the top of each candlestick, use a drill to bore a 1-inch-deep hole large enough in diameter for your candles. Drip a small amount of melted wax into each hole. Insert candles while wax is still warm.

Moss and Bark Wreath

Shown on page 67.
Finished wreath is 14 inches in diameter.

MATERIALS

14-inch-diameter straw wreath
Natural materials gathered from woods and fields, such as sphagnum moss, lichen, leaves, sticks, twigs, and tree bark
Wood glue or a hot-glue gun
Straight pins
Florist's wire

INSTRUCTIONS

Glue and pin moss to the front of the wreath, covering the straw.

Cover wreath with scraps of tree bark. Use a hot-glue gun or strong commercial wood glue and pins to hold bark in place. Using florist's wire, attach any large bark pieces that won't adhere with the glue.

Cover the bark ends and any exposed pins and wire with additional moss. Glue and pin lichen onto the bark pieces.

Glue twigs atop the wreath in a pleasing pattern, hiding the twig ends under other pieces whenever possible. If desired, glue leaves onto the wreath, using them to create visual balance.

Decorate the wreath with a velvet beaded star (see instructions, page 72) or add a ribbon bow. Attach the star or bow with florist's wire.

Twist florist's wire around a tying cord on the wreath, and form the wire into a hanging loop.

Velvet Star Ornaments

Shown on pages 64 and 67.
Finished stars are 5 inches across.

MATERIALS

Scraps of velveteen fabric in assorted colors
Polyester fiberfill
Large gold bead or ¼-inch-diameter gold button for each star center
Glass seed beads in assorted colors
15 glass bugle beads for each star
Very fine, medium-length beading needles
Gold thread
Cardboard or plastic for template

INSTRUCTIONS

Make a template from cardboard or plastic for the star pattern, *below.* Draw two stars onto the wrong side of the velveteen. Cut out the stars, adding ¼-inch seam allowances.

With *right* sides together, sew the star front to the star back, leaving a 1-inch opening along the side of one point for turning. Trim the seam allowance at the star points. At the inner angles, clip into the seam allowance almost to stitching. Turn the star right side out and stuff it firmly with fiberfill. Slip-stitch the opening closed.

Find the center of the star. Run a doubled sewing thread three or four times from front to back at the star center. Pull up the thread, creating a slight depression. Sew a large gold bead or button at the star center. Anchor thread firmly in the fabric; break off.

The technique for attaching beads is as follows: Place three to five beads on a beading needle at a time. Slide the beads into place and secure them with a small backstitch, going through one or two beads a second time. Do not pull the thread too tightly or the beads will pucker. Repeat until all the beads in the row are secured to the fabric.

Refer to the photograph, page 67, and the pattern, *below,* for placement of beads; blue lines on the pattern indicate the beading design. Use beads in colors that contrast with the background fabric. To keep the design symmetrical, work outward from the center of the star.

To begin, attach two circles of beads around large center bead. Then add long lines of beads along radiating lines indicated on pattern. Sew on nine beads of one color and finish with three beads of a second color. Sew 10 long lines.

Sew shorter lines of beads between the longer lines, attaching five beads of one color followed by three beads of a second color.

Work a small bird's-foot motif in each point of the star, referring to the photograph for the design. Start with a stem of five beads. Using one bugle bead and one bead of a contrasting color for each "toe," form three toes.

To finish the star, stitch a single row of beads along the seam around the star's perimeter.

VELVET STAR ORNAMENT

Fold

Beaded Stocking

Shown on page 66.
Finished stocking is approximately 22½ inches long.

MATERIALS

30x30-inch piece of 14-count needlepoint canvas
Tapestry needles
Paternayan 3-ply Persian wool yarn in the following colors: No. 742 gold, No. 643 olive, No. 641 dark olive, No. 431 medium brown, No. 424 light brown, No. 430 dark brown, No. 200 dark gray, No. 201 medium gray, No. 260 white, No. 203 light gray, No. 220 black, No. 445 beige, and No. 860 rust (background)
Gold metallic thread
Silver metallic thread
⅔ yard of fusible interfacing
¾ yard of white wool
1 yard of muslin
2½ yards of ⅜-inch-diameter gold rope trim
Clear nylon thread
Beading needle and thread
Approximately 1,600 plain black beads
Approximately 200 black faceted beads
Approximately 200 pearl white seed beads
Masking tape

INSTRUCTIONS

Tape canvas edges with masking tape to prevent fraying. Mark a beginning point for stitching in the lower-left corner of the canvas, 5½ inches from left edge and 3½ inches up from bottom. For stitching, use one ply of yarn; work the flowers in continental stitches and the background in basket-weave stitches (to minimize distortion).

Working from the chart, *opposite,* begin stitching at the red arrow; work from A to B. The stitching area is defined on the chart with black lines; work rust stitches in the background area encompassed by the
continued

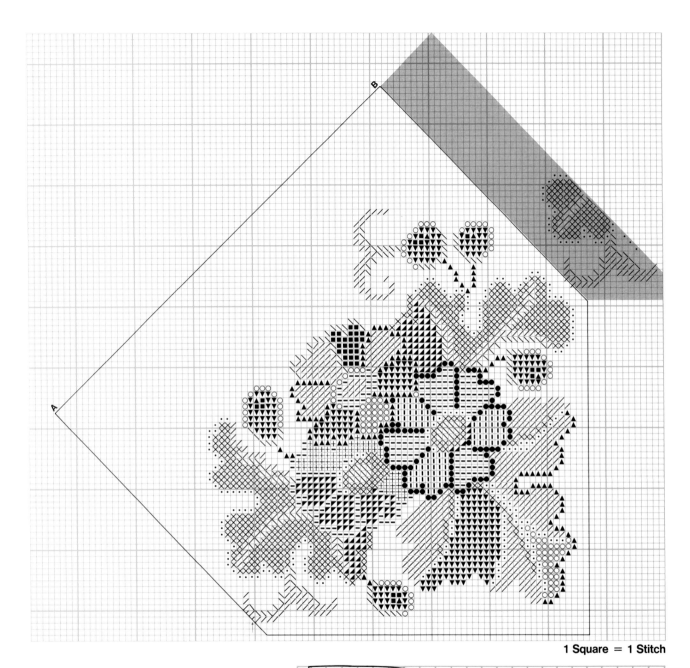

1 Square = 1 Stitch

COLOR KEY

⊡ Gold 742	◤ Medium Gray 201
⊠ Olive 643	○ White 260
◪ Dark Olive 641	▼ Light Gray 203
◉ Medium Brown 431	◼ Black 220
⊟ Light Brown 424	▲ Metallic Gold
⊡ Dark Brown 430	◩ Metallic Silver
⊞ Dark Gray 200	◿ Beige 445

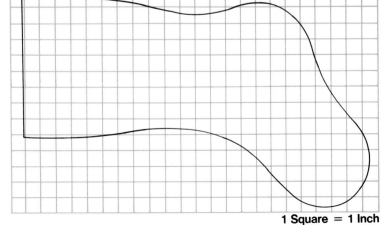

1 Square = 1 Inch

black lines. Repeat the design three more times (four total).

The design runs diagonally from the lower-left corner to the upper-right corner of the canvas.

Steam-press the completed needlepoint, using a medium-hot iron and a damp press-cloth.

To secure the needlepoint, machine-zigzag-stitch (using a narrow-width stitch) around the outer edge, barely catching last row of stitches. Trim canvas, leaving ½-inch seam allowance beyond the design.

For backing, fuse interfacing to a 10x24-inch piece of muslin. Cut interfaced muslin to the shape of the needlepoint.

Sew together the ends of the needlepoint, right sides facing, forming a circular cuff. Turn under and tack the lower-edge seam allowance, using clear thread and clipping as necessary. Repeat for muslin backing, treating the interfaced side of the muslin as the wrong side.

Hand-sew the needlepoint and backing together at the lower edge, wrong sides together. Baste upper cuff edges together.

Enlarge stocking pattern, page 73. Cut two stockings from white wool, adding ½-inch seam allowances. Cut two from muslin for lining.

Pin the right sides of the wool stockings together; sew around the stocking, leaving the top edge open. Clip the curves; turn and press. Repeat for the lining pieces, leaving a 6-inch opening at the bottom edge.

Slip the cuff over the stocking, with the *wrong* side of cuff facing the *right* side of stocking. Baste along the top edge, easing as necessary. Slip the stocking with the cuff into the lining, with *right* sides together and seams matching. Stitch around the top, through all layers. Clip and trim seam allowances.

To turn the stocking right side out, pull the stocking through the opening in the lining. Sew opening in lining closed. Press lining to the inside. With cuff turned up, sew through stocking and lining, ¼ inch from the cuff seam, to secure the lining to the stocking. Turn the cuff down over the stocking.

Hand-sew roping around the cuff top and along the stocking seams.

Sew beaded fringe to the cuff bottom. Use eight plain beads, one faceted bead, and one pearl white seed bead for each strand of fringe. Space strands two to three needlepoint stitches apart.

Beaded Sweater

Shown on page 68.
Directions are for Small (12); changes for Medium (14–16) and Large (18) follow in parentheses. Finished bust measurement: 36 (38, 40) inches.

MATERIALS

Aarlan Royal 50-g skeins: 5 (5, 6) No. 4319 red (A) and 7 (7, 8) skeins No. 4322 black (B)
Size 3 circular knitting needles (16- and 29-inch lengths)
Size 3 double-pointed needles
Size 5 circular knitting needles (11-, 16-, and 29-inch lengths) or size to obtain gauge given below
1,500 four-mm faceted opaque white beads; 130 eight-mm faceted opaque white beads
120 black seed beads
White bead thread; bead needle
Tapestry needle to fit through 4-mm and 8-mm beads when threaded with yarn

Abbreviations: See page 29.
Gauge: With larger needles over st st, 6 sts = 1 inch; 8 rows = 1 inch

INSTRUCTIONS

Note: This garment is constructed in the traditional fair isle manner of working the body in a tube from cast-on to shoulder without armhole openings. Each sleeve is worked separately in a tube to underarm length. Armhole openings are machine-stitched for stability, then cut open. Sleeves are set in.

When changing yarn colors in two-color (or fair isle) knitting, twist new color around color in use to prevent holes. Carry unused color loosely across back, twisting it every three or four stitches.

TO KNIT WITH BEADS: Insert right needle tip into back loop of stitch; slide bead up behind needle. With right needle tip, pick up thread just beyond bead and pull bead and thread through stitch, keeping bead on front of stitch and pushed down.

BODY: With B and smaller circular needle (29-inch length), cast on 216 (224, 234) sts. Join, being careful not to twist stitches. Place marker for beg of rnd. Working in rnds, * k 1 through back loop (tbl), p 1. Rep from * around. Continue in rib as established until length measures 2 inches, inc 4 (6, 6) sts on last rnd—220 (230, 240) sts.

Change to larger 29-inch-long needle. From here on, knit every rnd; work even for 1 rnd. Break off B. String 36 four-mm white beads on B.

Join B, beg Chart 1, *opposite,* rep between A and B around and working 4 petals of third (fourth, fourth) motif with beads, keeping center 4 sts of motif unbeaded. (See instructions, above.) Work until 17 rnds of Chart 1 are completed; on last rnd of Chart 1 dec 2 sts for Small, work even for Medium, inc 2 sts on Large: 218 (230, 242) sts.

Next rnd: Beg Chart 2 as follows: * Beg at A, work to C, then rep from B to C 16 (17, 18) times, then work from B to D. Place second marker; repeat from * once. Continue following Chart 2 pat as established until 6 rnds are completed. Rep these 6 rnds until total length measures 16 (16¼, 16½) inches or desired length to the underarm; end 4 sts before the first marker.

ARMHOLES: [Bind off next 4 sts, remove marker, bind off 8 more sts], continue in pat as established to 4 sts before second marker at right underarm. Rep bet [ ]s. Continue across back sts in pat as established—97 (103, 109) sts each Front and Back.

Rnd 2: With B cast on 2 sts, place marker, cast on 2 sts more with B, work in pat across sts of front to other armhole, cast on 2 sts with B, place marker, cast on 2 sts more with B and work in pat to end of rnd—202 (214, 226) sts.

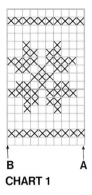

CHART 1

B   A

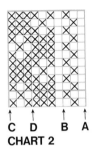

C   D   B   A

CHART 2

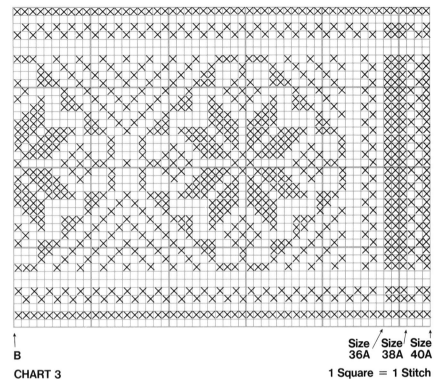

B

CHART 3

Size / Size / Size
36A   38A   40A

1 Square = 1 Stitch

Note: From this point on, work around the sweater body, working the 2 sts each side of both markers in reverse st st (purl these sts) with B. This is the cutting ridge for slashing open the armholes later. Continue in pat for approximately 1 (1½, 2) inch(es) more; end with Rnd 3 or 6.

Break off B and string 268 four-mm beads onto B; join B.

Keeping 4 reverse st sts in B at each armhole as before, work remaining sts following Chart 3 as follows: Begin at point indicated for each size, work from A to C, then from point B back to A. Continue to follow Chart 3 as established, working first large star motif in beads as shown in photo. When Chart 3 is completed, rep Chart 2 as previously established. Break off B.

NECK SHAPING: At the same time Rnd 34 of Chart 3 is completed, break off B. Sl first 44 (47, 50) sts of rnd to right needle without knitting; sl next 13 sts to holder for front neck. Join B; complete rnd, then work first 44 (47, 50) sts of rnd, ending at left neck edge. Working back and forth in rows [bind off 3 sts at

neck edge, complete row] 4 times, [bind off 2 sts at neck edge, complete row] 2 (2, 4) times, then [dec 1 st at neck edge, complete row] 4 times—169 (181, 189) sts. Work even until length from beg of armhole shaping measures 9 (9½, 10) inches, ending with wrong side row.

SHOULDER: Sl 32 (35, 36) sts of right front shoulder to holder, bind off next 4 reverse st sts, sl 32 (35, 36) sts of right back shoulder to second holder, sl next 33 (33, 37) sts of back to third holder for back of neck, sl next 32 (35, 36) sts to fourth holder for back left shoulder, bind off next 4 rev st sts and sl rem 32 (35, 36) sts to fifth holder for left front shoulder.

Break off all yarns. Machine-sew (zigzag or overcast stitches) down each side of cutting ridge at each armhole as close as possible to, but not into, the first st st. Cut between the rows of machine sewing. Weave shoulder with kitchner stitch.

NECKBAND: With smaller 16-inch-long circular needles, k 33 (33, 37) back neck sts from holder, pick up 22 (24, 26) sts along left neck edge, k

13 front neck sts from holder, pick up 22 (24, 26) sts along right neck edge. Place marker and join 90 (94, 102) sts. Work k 1 tbl, p 1 ribbing as for lower edge for 1¼ inch. Bind off stitches loosely.

SLEEVE: With smaller double-pointed needles, cast on 40 (44, 48) sts and join, being careful not to twist sts. Place marker for beg of round. Work in k 1 tbl, p 1 ribbing as for lower edge of body until length measures 3 inches, inc to 60 (70, 80) sts evenly spaced on last ribbing round.

Change to larger circular needle (11-inch length). Work Chart 1; inc 4 (6, 2) sts evenly spaced on last rnd of Chart 1, end 2 sts before the marker—64 (76, 82) sts. Keeping 2 sts each side of marker in "seam" pat as bet A and B of Chart 2, work rem sts in Chart 2 pat, rep bet B and C.

At the same time, keeping to Chart 2 pat as established, inc 1 st each side of "seam" pat sts every 4 (5, 6) rows 22 (20, 19) times, working inc sts in pat and changing to 16-inch-length needle as sts become crowded—109 (115, 121) sts.

continued

Work even until the total sleeve length measures 18 (19, 20) inches. Break off A. With B, work even 1 rnd. Work in k 1, p 1 rib for 5 rnds to form the sleeve facing. Bind off the stitches very loosely.

Make second sleeve, working petals of fourth motif of Chart 1 in beads as on body. Sew sleeves into armhole, using first st st after machine stitching on body and k round of B before ribbing of the sleeve. Leave the 5 rnds of ribbing free.

After the sleeve is sewn into the armhole, fold over 5 rounds of ribbing to cover the machine stitching. Loosely whipstitch the ribbing to the body section.

FOR YOKE FRINGE: To make the long fringe, secure thread on the wrong side in the first stitch of the solid black row at the lower-right corner of the yoke with a bead needle and thread. Bring the thread to the right side of the work and string five 4-mm beads, one 8-mm bead, and one 4-mm bead.

Skipping the last bead strung, run needle and thread back through the remaining beads to the wrong side of work, then back to the right side in the next stitch to left.

To make the short fringe, string five 4-mm beads and one black seed bead; skipping the last bead strung, run needle and thread back through the remaining beads to the wrong side of the work, then back to the right side of the work in the next stitch to the left.

Alternate long and short fringe, working across to left side of yoke. Continue to left shoulder line; fasten off. Repeat to make a second row of fringe, alternating long and short fringe from left shoulder line to right shoulder line.

The back of the sweater may be fringed if desired, but additional beads will be required.

Note: Do not dry-clean. Hand-wash only.

Eskimo Dolls

Shown on page 69.
Finished adult dolls are 14 inches tall; child doll is 11 inches tall.

MATERIALS
For each doll
Scraps of tan velveteen for face
Scraps of black velveteen for hair
Scraps of velveteen for clothing
Scraps of textured fabrics for
  animals
Scraps of white pile fabric for
  hood
1 yard of decorative trim
Buttons or beads for animal eyes
Pink permanent felt-tip marker
Black, white, brown, and red
  embroidery floss
Polyester fiberfill; tracing paper

INSTRUCTIONS
Trace the doll patterns, *below,* and on pages 77–79. The doll body patterns include ¼-inch seam allowances. The appliqué patterns for the animals, doll faces, hood, and hair are finished size and do not include seam allowances.

From the tan velveteen, cut the doll faces.

From the clothing fabrics, cut the pieces for the doll bodies and clothing. Cut two 4x5-inch pieces for the legs for *each* adult doll; cut two 3¼x4¾-inch pieces for the child's legs. Cut a 4x18-inch piece for the woman's skirt.

Cut hair for the dolls from the black velveteen.

To make one doll, appliqué face to doll front. Using embroidery floss, embroider facial features. Draw on cheeks with pink marker.

Appliqué the hair at the top of the face. Appliqué the white pile fabric around the face for a hood.

Choose an animal motif for doll front. Cut out and appliqué an animal onto front. Add seam allowances if hand appliquéing. Hand- or machine-embroider the stitching details. For the fish, use a zigzag stitch for the scales. For the owl and the fish, sew on beads or buttons for the eyes. For the seal, attach a bead nose; stitch the whiskers and eye using embroidery stitches.

With *right* sides facing, sew the center back seam from the top edge to the upper dot only. Sew the front to the back along side seams and around the head.

For Father and Child, sew trim around the body, 2 inches from the bottom edge; sew pile ½ inch from the bottom edge.

For Mother, hem the bottom skirt edge; make shallow pleats every 1½ inches around the skirt waist. Sew the skirt to the bottom edge of Mother; stitch trim around the waist at the skirt top to cover the seam.

Stitch the center back seam from the bottom edge to the lower dot, leaving an opening for turning and stuffing. Sew the torso base to the bottom edge. Turn the body right side out and stuff firmly. Slip-stitch the opening closed.

To make the arms, sew a mitten to the end of each arm. Sew the outer arm seam from the shoulder to the fingertips. Sew trim to the sleeve edge; sew pile below the trim at the wrist. Sew the remainder of the arm seam. Turn and stuff the arms. Sew the arms to the body, turning under the raw edges.

Sew the boots from the top to the dot along the front seam line. Sew the boots to the legs; sew on trim at the top of the boots. Stitch the remainder of the boot seam and continue up the back leg seam. Turn and stuff. Sew the legs to the body, turning under the raw edges.

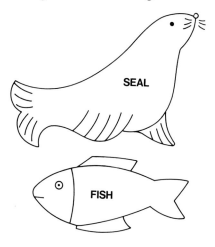

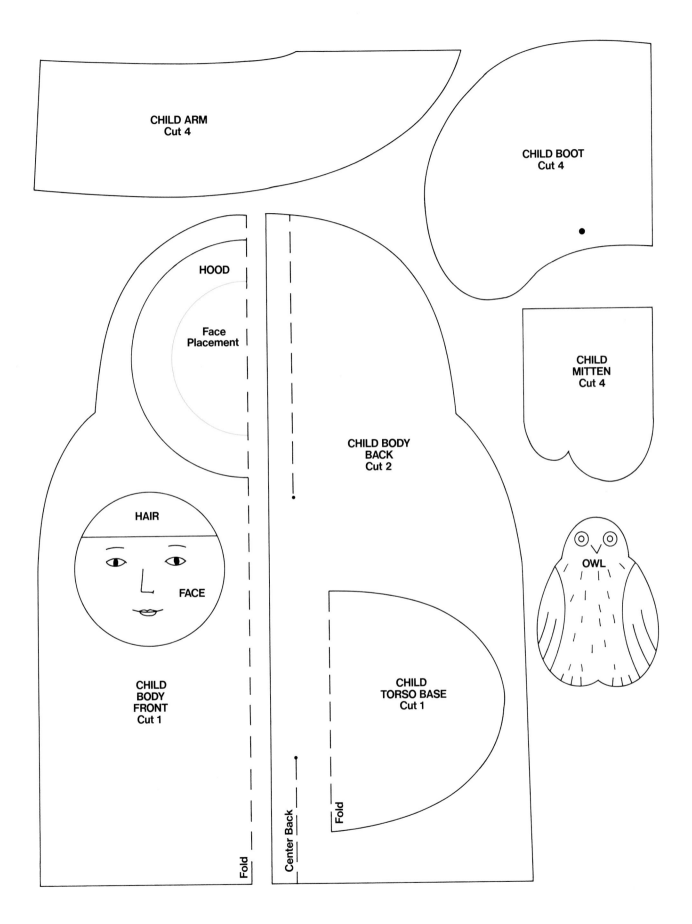

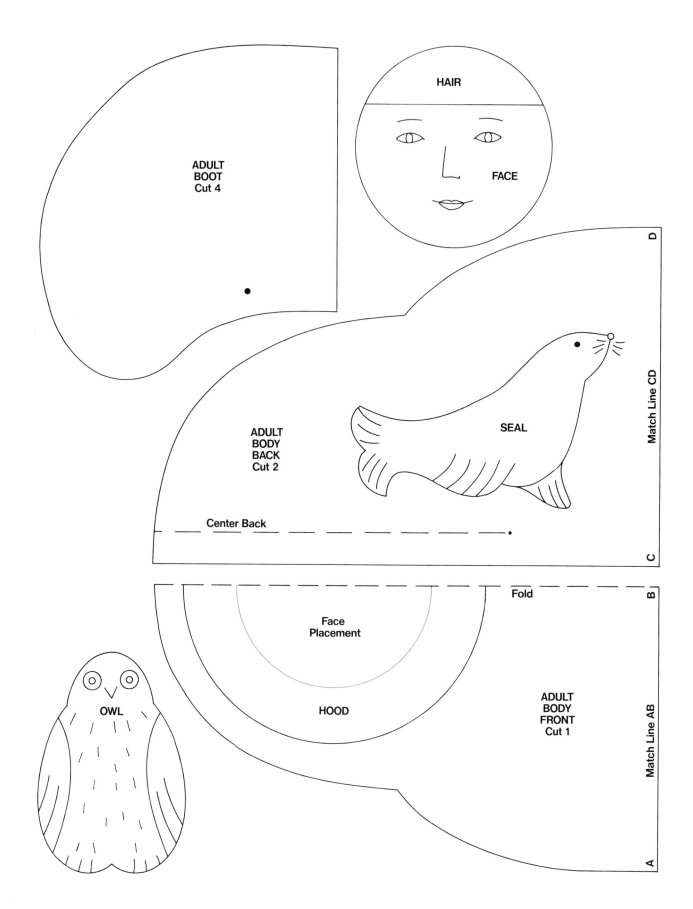

ADULT
BOOT
Cut 4

HAIR

FACE

D

Match Line CD

SEAL

ADULT
BODY
BACK
Cut 2

Center Back

C

Fold

B

Face
Placement

HOOD

ADULT
BODY
FRONT
Cut 1

Match Line AB

OWL

A

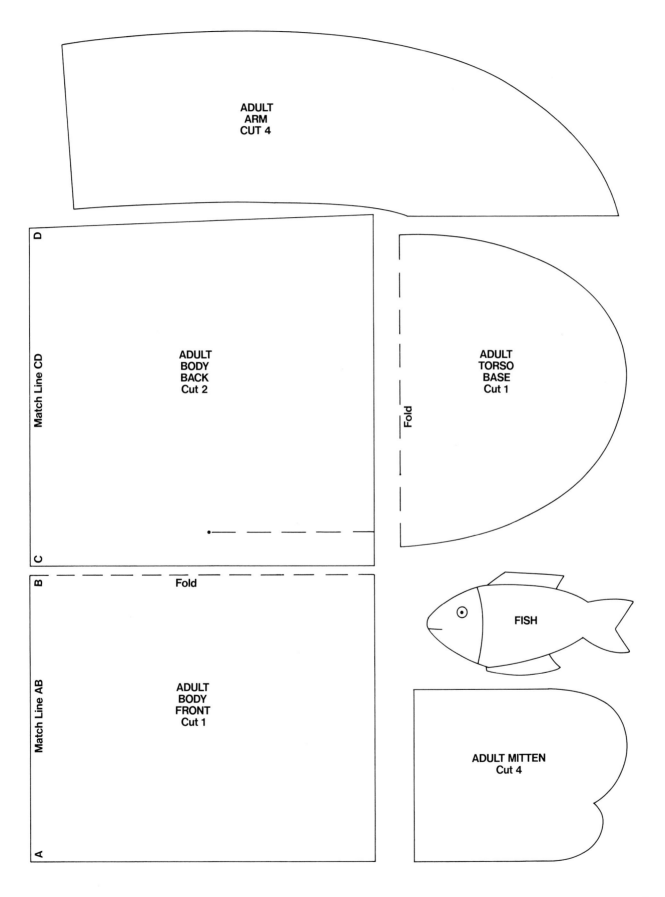

ADULT
ARM
CUT 4

D

Match Line CD

ADULT
BODY
BACK
Cut 2

C

ADULT
TORSO
BASE
Cut 1

Fold

B   Fold

Match Line AB

ADULT
BODY
FRONT
Cut 1

A

FISH

ADULT MITTEN
Cut 4

Christmas Patchwork Gifts and Trims

Traditional quilt patterns are timeless, and many of them lend themselves to imaginative adaptations for the holidays. The Tree of Life design, shown here on an antique quilt, is a perfect motif for a Christmas coverlet and seasonal trims and gifts such as place mats, stockings, and tree ornaments.

This 91½-inch-square antique quilt features 25 pieced blocks, each with 98 small triangles. (Piece the triangles individually, or use the quick-piecing method explained on page 92.)

The striking border (shown at left) was appliquéd to the quilt's border. We've simplified the border so you can piece it quickly and easily.

Instructions for the projects in this chapter begin on page 86.

Dear Santa, we hope you like them.
Merry Christmas
Love Lillian
and Mary Clare

Set a beautiful table at Christmas or anytime with this 15x54-inch runner and these 13x18-inch place mats inspired by the border on the Tree of Life quilt.

For the holidays, stitch these table toppers in red and white. For year-round use, stitch them in colors to complement your dishware or decor.

A cross-stitched Tree of Life ornament, *below,* makes a lively trim for your Christmas tree or for an evergreen wreath. For variety, sew the cross-stitch design into a scent bag to hang on the tree or in a closet. Stuff the bag with pine needles to remember the smells of Christmas throughout the year.

Time-honored quilt patterns lend themselves to many uses and a variety of crafting techniques. Here we've adapted just a portion of the Tree of Life design for pieced table linens, and translated the block motif into cross-stitches for a Christmas tree ornament.

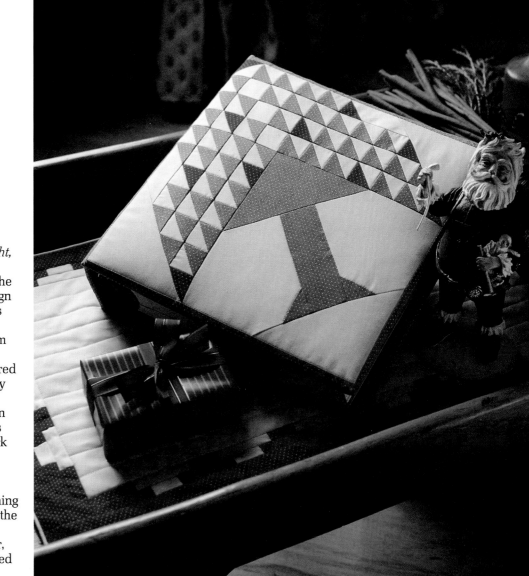

On the holiday photograph album, *right,* we've substituted red triangles for some of the green ones in the design to represent Christmas tree ornaments. To personalize your album cover, and make it a family tree, include a red triangle for each family member.

The triangles used in the Tree of Life blocks are ideal for patchwork Christmas stockings, *opposite.* Adapted for cross-stitch, the quilt border makes a charming cuff, particularly with the addition of a holiday greeting or a name. Or, sew a stocking accented with a pieced cuff.

For a treasured family gift, craft a Christmas album. By reserving it for snapshots and other mementos of each year's celebration, eventually you'll have a pictorial—and uniquely personal—history of your family's festivities to share with loved ones. Assemble the stockings using triangles from the Tree of Life pattern and a cross-stitch adaptation of the quilt border.

Tree of Life Quilt

Shown on pages 80 and 81.
Finished quilt is 91½x91½ inches.

MATERIALS

All fabrics are 45-inch-wide cotton
   broadcloth
7½ yards of muslin for piecing
5 yards of solid red fabric
¾ yard of muslin for binding
9 yards of backing fabric
Quilt batting larger than 92 inches
   square
Water-erasable marking pen
Cardboard or template plastic

INSTRUCTIONS

This quilt consists of 25 pieced
blocks combined with plain blocks
and triangles. We simplified the border, which was painstakingly appliquéd on the original quilt, so you
can piece it to complete the top.

In the branch portion of each Tree
of Life block, there are 98 small triangles. These triangles may be cut
and pieced individually or stitched
in groups, using the quick-piecing
method explained on page 92.

TO BEGIN: Trace the patterns, *opposite,* and make cardboard or plastic templates.

For the setting squares and triangles, make an 11-inch-square template from cardboard or plastic.

Note: The patterns are finished
size and *do not* include seam allowances. Add ¼-inch seam allowances to all pieces before cutting
them from fabric.

CUTTING INSTRUCTIONS: Wash
and press all fabric to preshrink it
and to remove any sizing before cutting out pieces.

Adding ¼-inch seam allowances,
use the 11-inch-square template to
mark and cut 16 setting squares
from muslin. (The cut squares will
measure 11½ inches square.) Set
the squares aside.

For the setting triangles, draw a
diagonal line between opposite cor-

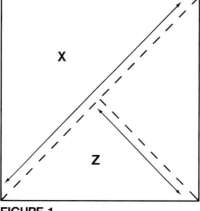

FIGURE 1

ners of the template used for marking the setting squares. Draw a
second diagonal line in the *opposite*
direction, through the lower section
of the template (see Figure 1, *above*).
Cut on the drawn lines to form templates X and Z.

Using template X, mark 16 setting
triangles on the muslin with the *long*

side of the triangle template on the
straight of the fabric grain. Adding
¼-inch seam allowances, cut out
the triangles.

Next, using template Z, mark four
corner-setting triangles on the muslin, with the legs of the triangle template on the straight of the fabric
grain. Adding seam allowances, cut
out the triangles. Set the X and Z
triangles aside.

For the 25 pattern blocks, use templates A, B, C, D, E, and F (add seam
allowances). The number to cut for
the entire quilt is listed first, followed by the number to cut for one
block (in parentheses). Or, follow
the quick-piecing method explained
on page 92.

From the remaining muslin, cut
pieces as follows: 1,125 (45) of piece
A, 75 (3) *each* of pieces B and C, and
50 (2) *each* of pieces E and F (reverse the templates for half of the E
and F pieces).

continued

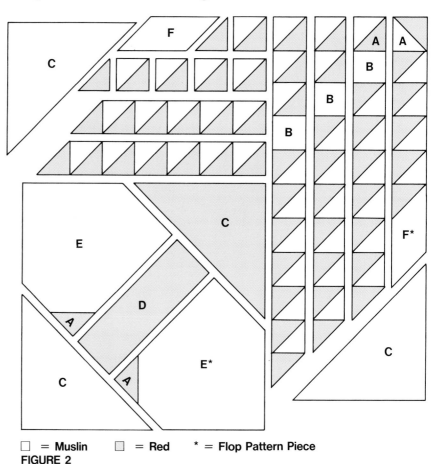

☐ = Muslin   ☐ = Red   * = Flop Pattern Piece
FIGURE 2

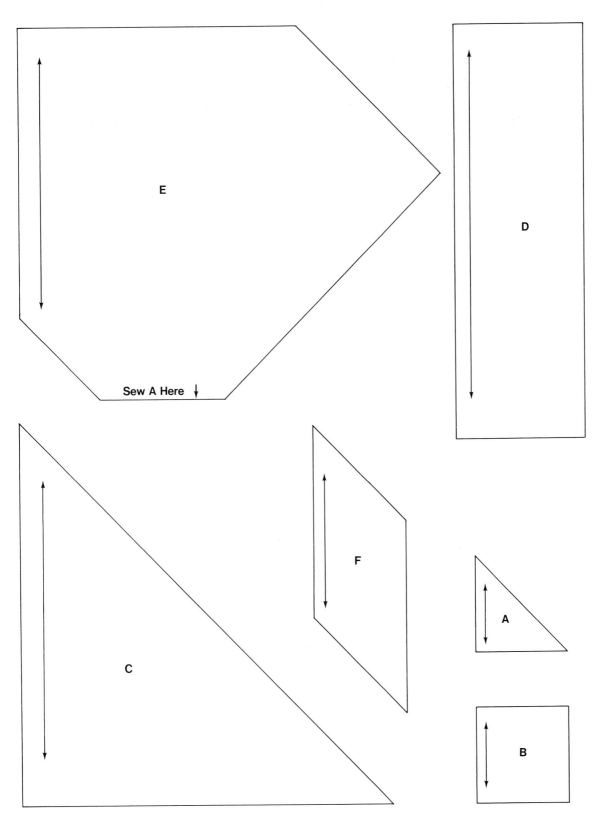

E

Sew A Here ↓

D

C

F

A

B

PATCHWORK TEMPLATE PATTERNS

From the red fabric, cut pieces as follows: 1,375 (55) of piece A and 25 (1) *each* of pieces C and D.

TO PIECE THE BLOCKS: Assemble each block by hand or machine, following the block piecing diagram (Figure 2) on page 86. As you stitch each block unit, press seams to one side (toward the darker fabric).

Make 25 Tree of Life blocks.

FOR THE INNER QUILT TOP: Before stitching the top of your quilt together, you may want to use a water-erasable marking pen to mark the quilting designs on the setting squares and triangles.

Trace the block quilting design on pages 90–91 onto tracing paper. Add the extra petal quilting designs in the positions indicated on the pattern to complete the design. Darken the quilting lines on the pattern sheet with a black marker to make them easier to see. Using a water-erasable marking pen, trace the quilting design onto the setting squares. Trace half of the design onto the setting triangles.

If it is difficult to see the quilting pattern lines through the fabric, use a light box to make tracing through the fabric easier. If you do not have a light box, you can easily create a "light box" effect at a window in the daytime. Tape the traced pattern to a window; tape the fabric over the pattern. Because the light shines through the pattern and the fabric, you can see to trace on most fabrics, even very dark ones.

Then, set the pieced and plain blocks together in diagonal rows, as shown *below*. The shaded blocks on the diagram represent the pieced blocks. The inner quilt top (without border) should measure 78 inches square, including seam allowances.

FOR THE BORDERS: To cut and piece the border units, refer to Figures 4 and 5, *opposite. Note:* Dimensions in the diagrams are *finished* sizes; add ¼-inch seam allowances when cutting the strips for piecing. Make 20 border units and four corner units.

To assemble the borders, refer to Figure 6, *opposite.* Join together five border units for each of the four borders. Next, sew a five-unit border to two opposite sides of the quilt top. Sew corner units to each end of the remaining borders, making sure the corners turn correctly. Stitch these long border strips to the remaining two sides of the quilt top.

Trace the patterns for the border quilting design and border corner quilting design on page 91. Using a water-erasable marking pen, trace a border corner design onto the white area of each corner. Trace the border quilting design twice on each pieced border section, making the design flow around the quilt.

FINISHING: Cut and piece fabric for the back of your quilt. Divide backing fabric into three 3-yard lengths. Cut or tear one length so it is 21 inches wide. Sew a full panel to each side of the narrow panel, using ½-inch seams. Cut off the selvages to leave about ¼-inch seam margins. Press the seams to one side.

Layer quilt top, batting, and backing. Pin, baste all layers, and quilt.

When quilting is complete, trim the excess batting and quilt back even with the quilt top.

Bind the outer edges of the quilt. For binding, cut and piece approximately 390 inches of 1¼-inch-wide muslin bias strips. Stitch the binding to the quilt top (¼-inch seam), mitering the corners. Turn under the remaining raw edge of the binding ¼ inch. Fold the binding to the quilt back, covering the previous stitching, and blindstitch the binding to the quilt back.

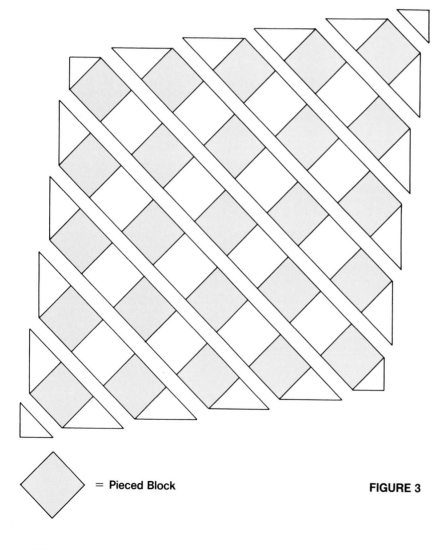

◇ = Pieced Block

FIGURE 3

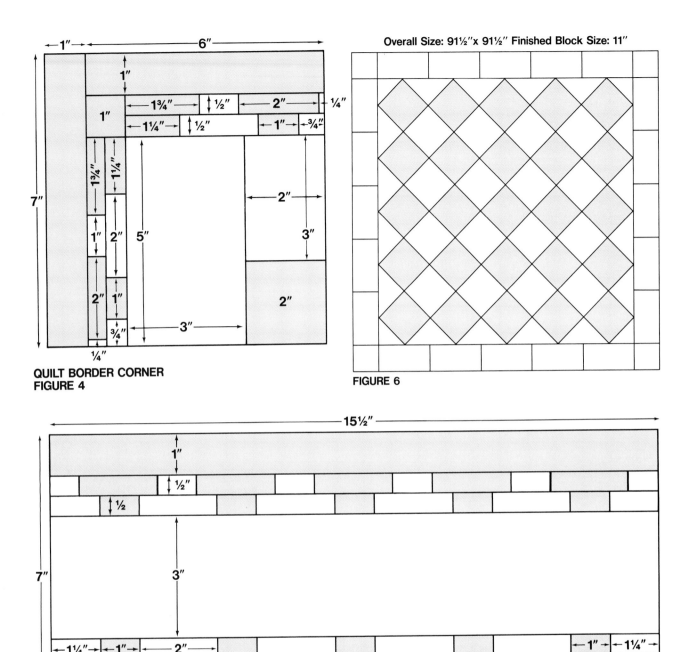

Overall Size: 91½"x 91½" Finished Block Size: 11"

QUILT BORDER CORNER
FIGURE 4

FIGURE 6

QUILT BORDER UNIT
FIGURE 5

89

Placement
for Petal

B

Match Line AB

A

PETAL
QUILTING
DESIGN

Placement
for Petal

QUILTING DESIGNS FOR BLOCKS

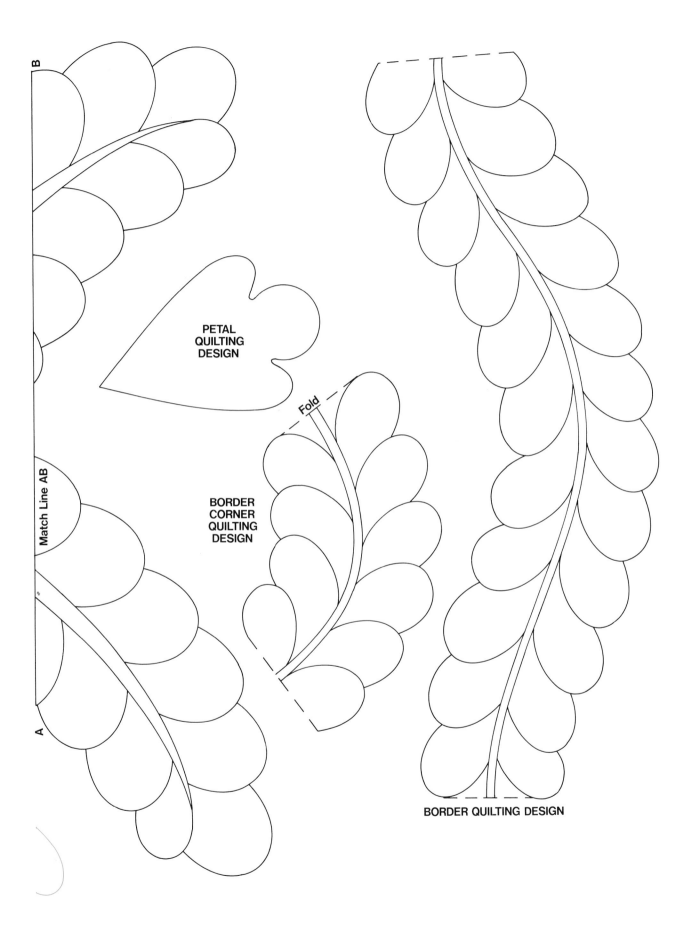

B

Match Line AB

A

PETAL
QUILTING
DESIGN

Fold

BORDER
CORNER
QUILTING
DESIGN

BORDER QUILTING DESIGN

91

QUICK-PIECING RIGHT-ANGLE TRIANGLES

The Tree of Life pattern calls for 98 small triangles in the branch portion of the design in each block. Ninety of the right-angle triangles are paired into 45 "triangle-squares" that can be machine-pieced. If you want to quickly piece these units, *do not* mark and cut the individual A pieces. Instead, follow the instructions below.

First, cut 23 squares of muslin, each 10x10 inches.

Then, cut 23 squares of red fabric, each 10x10 inches. Using triangle template A (pattern on page 87), mark triangles on the muslin as shown *below*. Allow at least ½ inch of space between the triangles for ¼-inch seams on all sides. Shaded area on the diagram denotes traced area; white area denotes seam allowances.

Place a marked muslin square atop a red square,

right sides facing. Press gently to help fabrics cling together. Machine-sew on the *diagonal sewing lines only* (dashed lines), as shown, then steam-press.

Finally, cut the triangles apart on the *cutting* lines. Open each triangle-square unit; press the seam toward the darker fabric. You will have 50 units, more than enough to piece one Tree of Life block.

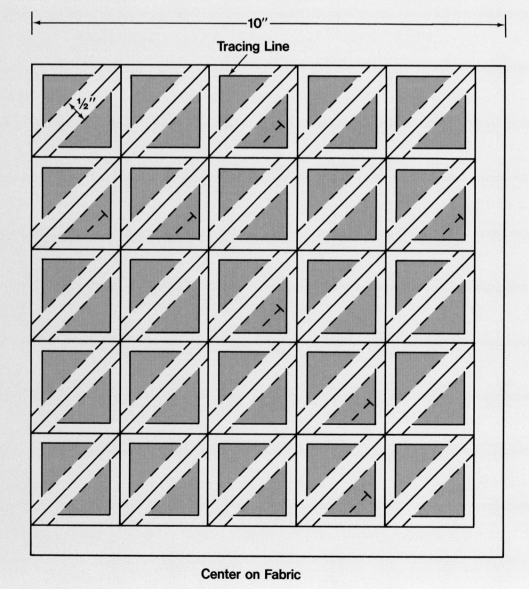

Center on Fabric

Table Runner
And Place Mats

Shown on pages 82 and 83.
Runner is 15x54 inches.
Place mats are 13x18 inches.

MATERIALS

For the table runner and two place mats

1½ yards of muslin or ecru fabric
1¾ yards of red pindot fabric
1⅝ yards of backing fabric
1½ yards of fleece
4 packages of oyster-color piping

INSTRUCTIONS

FOR THE TABLE RUNNER: On the lengthwise grain of fabric, cut pieces as follows from the red fabric (dimensions include ¼-inch seam allowances): forty-two 1x2½-inch A strips, thirty-four 1x1½-inch B strips, four 1½x1½-inch C pieces, two 1½x13½-inch D strips, two 1½x54½-inch E strips, and eight 1x2-inch F strips (inside row ends).

From the ecru fabric, cut thirty-eight 1x2½-inch G strips and thirty-eight 1x1½-inch H strips.

Use ¼-inch seam allowances to join the pieces. Referring to the table runner diagram, *right,* alternately sew A to H strips for the long side of the runner (17 A, 16 H). For the second (inside) row, alternately join B and G pieces; begin and end with F (F, 16 G, 15 B, F). Join the pieced strips lengthwise. Repeat to make the border for the opposite side.

Join the pieces for the runner ends in the same way. Add a red C square to each end.

For the runner center, cut 12x51-inch pieces of both the ecru fabric and the fleece. Mark lines 1 inch apart (lengthwise) for quilting.

Hand-baste the ecru fabric to the fleece. Machine-quilt along marked quilting lines. When the quilting is complete, trim the center piece to 11½x50½ inches.

continued

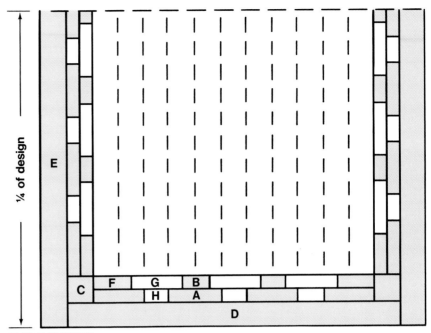

TABLE RUNNER

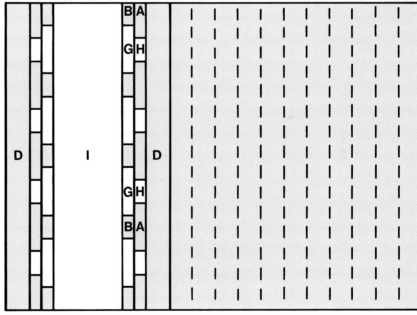

PLACE MAT

Sew the long pieced strips to the center; trim fleece from the seams. Sew the short pieced strips to the center; trim fleece from the seams.

Sew the D strips to the ends and the E strips to the sides. Baste piping to the seam line on the right side of the runner.

From the ecru fabric, cut backing to match the top. With *right* sides facing, sew the runner to the backing; leave an opening. Turn the runner right side out; press. Slip-stitch the opening closed.

FOR THE PLACE MATS: On the lengthwise grain of fabric, cut pieces as follows from the red fabric (dimensions include ¼-inch seam allowances): twenty 1x2½-inch A strips, twenty 1x1½-inch B strips, and two 1½x13½-inch D strips.

From the ecru fabric, cut pieces as follows: sixteen 1x2½-inch G strips, sixteen 1x1½-inch H strips, and one 3½x13½-inch I strip.

To make one mat, alternately join the A and H strips and the B and G strips, following the diagram at the bottom of page 93, to make four strips. Join pairs of strips; trim excess A strips on the ends (strips measure 13½ inches, including the seam allowances).

Join the two pieced strips lengthwise on the sides of the I strip. Sew the D strips to the sides.

Cut a piece of fleece 7x13½ inches; baste the patchwork on top. Machine-quilt the lengthwise seams.

Cut a 12x13½-inch piece from both the red fabric and the fleece (the long sides line up with the patchwork). Mark quilting lines 1 inch apart on the red piece. Baste the red piece atop the fleece; machine-quilt along the marked lines. Stitch the quilted red piece to the patchwork. Trim fleece from seam.

Baste piping to the seam line around the right side of the mat. From the ecru fabric, cut lining to match the top. Sew the top to the lining, leaving an opening. Turn, and sew the opening closed. Repeat to make a second place mat.

Cross-Stitch Tree Trim
Shown on page 83.
Ornament shown in photograph is 3¾ inches square.

MATERIALS
White or off-white hardanger or other even-weave fabric for embroidery, approximately 6½x6½ inches for each ornament
Scraps of white or off-white backing fabric, approximately 5x5 inches for each ornament
Red and green embroidery floss
Scraps of fleece or quilt batting
Fiberfill (optional)
Evergreen needles or potpourri
Narrow red ribbon

INSTRUCTIONS
Following chart, *opposite,* cross-stitch the design for the tree in green and for the border in red. Use two strands of floss and stitch over two threads of hardanger.

On hardanger, the complete design will be approximately 3¼ inches square before finishing. Stitched on other even-weave fabrics, the size of the motif will vary depending on the thread count and the number of threads over which you work the cross-stitches.

TO FINISH AS AN ORNAMENT OR A SACHET: Cut a 4½-inch-square piece of both fleece (or quilt batting) and backing fabric. Place the fleece or batting beneath the embroidered fabric. Centering it behind the design, baste to secure.

With *right* sides facing, machine-sew the embroidered fabric and the backing together approximately ¼ inch outside the cross-stitched border. Leave an opening for turning. Trim seams to ¼ inch, clip corners, and turn.

If desired, fill the "pillow" with cedar or pine needles or with fiberfill. Slip-stitch the opening closed. Tack a loop of narrow red ribbon to the top corner to use as a hanger.

TO FINISH AS A SCENT BAG: Sew the embroidered fabric to a scrap of backing fabric and stitch into a small bag. Stitch a narrow casing in the top of the bag for a drawstring or ribbon. Fill bag with needles or potpourri and draw the opening closed.

Holiday Album Cover
Shown on page 85.
Album shown in photograph is 12 inches square.

MATERIALS
Purchased photograph album (see note, *below*)
⅝ yard of green pindot fabric
½ yard of muslin
Scraps of red pindot fabric
Quilt batting
Spray adhesive
Fabric glue
Water-erasable marking pen

INSTRUCTIONS
Note: The patchwork block used for the album cover will be 11½ inches square (including seam allowances) before the border is added. Consequently, the album should be at least 11 inches square to accommodate the design. For an album larger than 11 inches square, or for a rectangular album (one side must be at least 11 inches long), increase the width of border strips.

TO BEGIN: Preshrink and press all fabrics. Make cardboard or plastic templates for the tree patterns on page 87. *Note:* The patterns are finished size and *do not* include seam allowances. Add ¼-inch seam allowances to all pieces before cutting them from fabric.

CUTTING INSTRUCTIONS: Mark and cut the pieces for one Tree of Life block as listed below. Or, use the quick-piecing method explained on page 92.

From the muslin, cut 42 A pieces, 3 B pieces, 3 C pieces, 2 E pieces,

COLOR KEY ■ Red ☒ Green

1 Square = 1 Stitch

and 2 F pieces (turn the templates over with wrong side up to reverse the templates when cutting the reverse E and F pieces).

From the red fabric scraps, cut nine A pieces.

From the green fabric, cut 46 A pieces and one *each* of piece C and piece D.

Note: If you alter the number of red squares and triangles in the patchwork block (to personalize the design), you'll need to recalculate the numbers of red and green triangles (A pieces) needed for the block.

TO PIECE THE BLOCK: Stitch the pieces together following the piecing diagram (Figure 2) included with the Tree of Life Quilt instructions on

page 86. Press seams toward the darker fabric as you go.

TO PREPARE THE COVER: For the borders, cut three strips of green pindot fabric wide enough to cover the album top, allowing enough for 1½ inches to tuck around the edge
continued

95

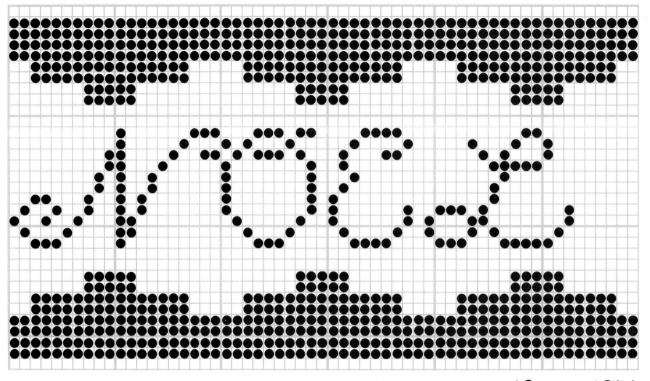

1 Square = 1 Stitch

of the front cover and for ¼-inch seams. (Our album is 12 inches square, so these strips are 2¼ inches wide and 13¾ inches long.)

Stitch the border strips to the top, bottom, and right-hand edges of the patchwork block (see the photograph on page 85). Leave the left-hand edge of the block, which will fall along the album spine, free. Miter or butt-join the border corners. Press the seams toward the borders.

Cut a piece of green fabric to cover the rest of the album (spine and back). The fabric piece should be the *width* of the patchwork, plus the top and bottom borders (measure along the left side), and the *length* needed to cover the spine and back, plus 1½ inches to tuck under and ¼ inch for seam. (On album shown, this piece measures 15x16¾ inches.)

TO FINISH THE COVER: Remove the pages from the album; spread the album flat, *right* side up. Cut a piece of batting the size of the flat album cover. Spray the outside of

the album with adhesive; lightly press the batting onto the surface with your hands to fix it in place.

Stitch the green fabric for the album back to the patchwork top along the left-hand edge.

Stretch the album cover around the album, securing the borders with fabric glue on the inside of the cover. Clip and trim the borders as necessary to fit them around the binder. Miter the border corners on the inside of the album cover.

For the lining, mark two pieces of muslin large enough to cover the raw edges of the border fabric on the inside front and back covers of the album. Add ¼-inch or ½-inch seam allowances on all sides except the side nearest the metal binder on the spine; cut out muslin.

To assemble, glue the lining close to the metal along the spine; then turn under and glue or slip-stitch the remaining lining edges in place so they cover the green borders and extend almost to the edges of the inside cover.

Christmas Stockings
Shown on page 84.
Stockings are 14 inches long.

MATERIALS
For each stocking
½ yard of fabric for stocking back and lining
½ yard of polyester fleece
1 package of white or red purchased piping
Cardboard or plastic for templates

For the stocking with the cross-stitched cuff
5x16-inch piece of hardanger fabric for the cuff
Red embroidery floss
¼ yard *each* of green and muslin fabrics for piecing triangle-squares

For the stocking with the pieced cuff
½ yard of red fabric for the stocking
Green and muslin fabric scraps for the cuff

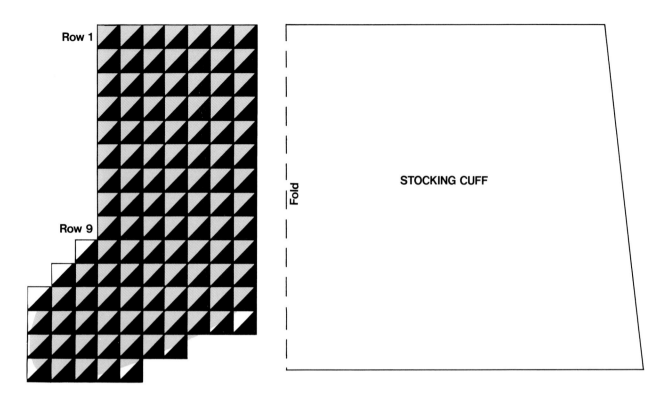

Row 1

Row 9

Fold

STOCKING CUFF

INSTRUCTIONS

For the stocking with the cross-stitched cuff

Make a template for triangle pattern A on page 87 for the Tree of Life Quilt. Pattern A is finished size; add ¼-inch seam allowances when cutting pieces from fabric.

Using template A, cut 105 triangles *each* from the green and the muslin fabrics. Sew pairs of green and white triangles into squares. Or, use the quick-piecing method explained on page 92 to piece right-angle triangles into 105 squares.

Referring to the diagram *above,* sew together squares to create fabric for the stocking front.

Enlarge the stocking pattern (on the diagram, *above*) on a 1-inch grid. Each triangle-square on the diagram equals 1 inch on the grid. Adding ¼-inch seam allowances, use the pattern to cut the stocking front from pieced fabric. Cut one stocking back and two lining pieces from muslin to match stocking front.

Back the stocking front and back with fleece. Baste piping along the

seam line around the sides and bottom of the stocking front.

Sew the back to the front, leaving the top open. Sew stocking lining in the same manner, leaving an opening along the stocking bottom.

Using three strands of embroidery floss, cross-stitch the cuff, referring to the chart, *opposite.* Work each stitch over two threads on the hardanger fabric. Extend stitched border design to fit around the top of the stocking.

Cut a cuff lining to match the cuff. Back the cuff with fleece. Sew piping to the top and bottom of the cuff. Sew the cuff into a loop and the cuff lining into a loop. Placing *right* sides together, sew the cuff to the cuff lining along the bottom edge; turn right side out.

Sew the cuff to the stocking, placing the *lining* side of the cuff together with the *right* side of the stocking.

Insert the stocking into the lining, *right* sides facing. Sew around the top of the stocking. Turn the stocking right side out through the hole in the lining; stitch the lining closed. Tuck the lining into the stocking.

For the stocking with pieced cuff

Enlarge the pattern for the stocking, *above,* as directed in the instructions for the stocking with the cross-stitched cuff, left.

Make a template for triangle pattern A on page 87 for the Tree of Life Quilt. Pattern A is finished size; add ¼-inch seam allowances when cutting fabric pieces.

Use template A to cut 56 triangles *each* from the green and the muslin fabrics. Stitch the green and muslin triangles together into 56 squares. Press the seam allowances toward the green fabric. Or, use the quick-piecing method explained on page 92 to piece right-angle triangles into 56 squares.

Piece triangle-squares to create fabric for the cuff. Make pieced fabric 14 triangle-squares wide and four triangle-squares deep.

Trace the cuff pattern, *above.* Cut two cuffs from the pieced fabric.

Assemble the cuff and stocking; follow instructions for the stocking with the cross-stitched cuff, left.

97

Good Scents

At Christmastime, nothing matches the enticing aroma of oranges, cinnamon, and cloves simmering gently on the stove, or the scent of freshly cut evergreens somewhere in the house. Here are some delightfully fragrant mixtures you can make at home.

This 15-inch-diameter cinnamon-stick wreath, *right,* combines pungent spices and fragrant herbs with colorful dried flowers. Directions are included for the wreath; follow the instructions on page 101 to dry your own flowers. Or, purchase dried flowers such as statice and yarrow at floral supply stores.

Spice Potpourri, the white mixture in the tray *opposite,* combines coarse salt and spices.

Clockwise from the Spice Potpourri are Woodland Potpourri, a mix of pinecones and spices; Pine Potpourri, a blend of pine needles and orange peels; and Christmas Simmer, a scented brew.

Cinnamon-Stick Wreath

Shown on pages 98 and 99.
Finished wreath is 15 inches
in diameter.

MATERIALS

13-inch-diameter cardboard circle
100 thick, 4- to 5-inch-long
　cinnamon sticks
Six bay leaves
Assorted dried flowers of various
　sizes and colors
White statice
Hot-glue gun

INSTRUCTIONS

To make the wreath base, cut an 8-inch-diameter circle from the center of the cardboard circle. Using a hot-glue gun, attach the cinnamon sticks around the cardboard circle, toward the outside.

Glue the white statice around the wreath center, extending it over the cinnamon sticks, almost covering the outer edge of the wreath. Glue a variety of dried flowers over the statice at the wreath center. Tuck the bay leaves under the statice and flowers and glue in place.

Spice Potpourri

Shown on page 99.

MATERIALS

3 pounds of coarse salt
½ cup *each* of whole allspice,
　cloves, and ginger
1 cup of broken cinnamon sticks
3 whole nutmegs

INSTRUCTIONS

Crush the nutmegs with a hammer. Mix the salt, crushed nutmegs, whole allspice, cloves, ginger, and cinnamon sticks in a large glass jar. Cover the jar with a lid.

Store the mixture for six weeks, until the salt is well seasoned. Pour the mix into small, lidded jars.

To scent a closet, remove the lid. Close the lid when not in use.

Woodland Potpourri

Shown on page 99.

MATERIALS

4 cups of small pinecones
10 anise stars
10 short cinnamon sticks
½ cup *each* of allspice, cloves,
　and orrisroot
10 bay leaves
10 drops of oil of cloves

INSTRUCTIONS

Drop the oil of cloves onto the orrisroot; set aside.

Gently mix the pinecones, anise stars, cinnamon sticks, allspice, cloves, and bay leaves in a large bowl. Add the oiled orrisroot granules to the mix.

Pour the mix into a large glass jar. Cover the jar and store the mix for six weeks. Shake the jar once every week to mix.

To scent the air, pour the mix into an open bowl. Place the bowl in a room where it can be enjoyed. Stir the mixture once a week to revive the scent.

Pine Potpourri

Shown on page 99.

MATERIALS

4 cups of dried pine needles
1 cup *each* of dried orange (or
　lemon) peel and rose petals
½ cup of broken cinnamon sticks
2 tablespoons of orrisroot
10 drops of oil of pine

INSTRUCTIONS

Drop the oil of pine onto the orrisroot; set aside.

Gently mix the pine needles, orange peel, rose petals, and cinnamon sticks in a large bowl. Add the oiled orrisroot granules to the mix.

Pour the mix into a large glass jar. Cover the jar. Store for six weeks, shaking the jar once every week to mix thoroughly.

To scent the air, pour the mix into an open bowl. Place the bowl in a room where it can be enjoyed. Stir the mixture once a week to revive the scent.

Christmas Simmer

Shown on page 99.

MATERIALS

1 cup *each* of whole allspice,
　broken cinnamon sticks, dried
　orange peel, bay leaves,
　coriander, and mint
½ cup *each* of whole cloves, star
　anise, pine needles, rosemary
　leaves, and orrisroot chips
15 drops of cinnamon oil
10 drops of clove oil
5 drops of orange oil

INSTRUCTIONS

Mix the cinnamon oil, clove oil, and orange oil with the orrisroot chips; set aside.

Blend the whole allspice, cinnamon sticks, orange peel, bay leaves, coriander, mint, cloves, anise, pine needles, and rosemary leaves in a large mixing bowl. Add the oil-soaked chips.

To scent the air, add ⅓ cup of mix to 4 cups of water in a cooking pot. Bring the mixture to a boil; lower heat. Simmer, adding more water as needed. The mixture may be refrigerated in a covered jar and reused.

MAKING POTPOURRI

Collect the dried petals of fragrant flowers, such as roses, lavender, and verbena. Combine the dried petals with spices, such as ground cloves, cinnamon, and orange or lemon peel, and mix well. Add orrisroot to the mixture as a fixative. If desired, add scented oils to orrisroot chips before adding the chips to the dried petals.

DRYING FRESH FLOWERS

Fresh flowers can be dried all year round, whenever they are available. Start by picking or buying a bouquet of your favorite blossoms. Zinnias, carnations, roses, black-eyed susans, daffodils, yarrows, pansies, and daisies can all be dried successfully. Keep in mind that the drying process tends to darken and intensify colors, so it's best to start with white, bright, or pastel flowers.

Drying with silica gel

Available in garden and hobby shops, silica gel can be used to absorb the moisture from flowers. The gel is a compound of sand-size crystals mixed with larger blue crystals. When the crystals are dry, the gel is blue; when they are damp, the gel turns pink. As long as the gel retains its blue color, it can be used again and again. When it turns pink, simply heat it in a warm oven until the pink crystals turn blue again.

To dry your flowers, you'll need airtight containers deep enough to hold the largest blooms. Trim the stem of each flower to about 1 inch.

Sprinkle a layer of silica gel into each container and place flowers (blossoms up) in rows so that about ½ inch of each stem is buried in gel. Add more crystals in and around blossoms until they are completely covered. Be careful not to distort the natural shapes of the flowers.

Cover and seal the containers; tape the edges around lids. Leave the containers in a dry, dark place for at least 10 days,

perhaps longer, depending on the size of the flowers. (Large blossoms usually require 12 to 14 days.)

After 10 days, check the flowers; the petals should be dry but not brittle. If the petals still feel fresh and supple, continue to check the flowers every two or three days.

When the flowers are dry, carefully remove them from the silica gel; then gently shake the crystals from the flower petals.

Drying in a microwave

Drying flowers with silica gel in a microwave oven is much faster and preserves the color and shape of the blooms much better than conventional drying.

Trim flower stems to within 1 inch of each flower. Pour about 1½ inches of silica gel or a mixture of two parts cornmeal to one part borax into a microwavable container. The container should be large enough to afford 2 inches between the top layer of gel and the top of the bowl to allow for expansion of the gel during heating.

Place a single flower in the bowl, blossom up. Gently add gel granules until the bloom is *completely* covered.

Pour 8 ounces of water into a measuring cup or other glass container. Place the water in one corner of the microwave oven. Put the gel-covered flower in the oven. *Do not cover the container.* Dry one flower at a time.

Drying times range from several seconds to three minutes, depending on the bloom's size and texture, on

whether you use gel or the cornmeal and borax mixture, and on your oven's heating capacity. Experiment with different times. The color of the gel will change from blue to pink as moisture is absorbed and the flower dries.

When flower is dried, remove container from oven and set it on newspaper. *Don't touch the gel.* Allow it to cool for 20 minutes.

Pour off the top layer of gel. Gently lift out the flower, which will be limp, and place it on top of the remaining gel in the bowl. Let the flower rest until it is firm enough to handle (5 to 20 minutes).

When the flower is firm, *gently* remove the remaining gel with an artist's brush. Place the dried bloom atop a container of cool gel. Allow it to rest overnight until it is firm and easy to handle. The cold gel can be reused to dry other materials.

Using dried blossoms

When you are ready to arrange the flowers, attach florist's wire to the stems with twists of floral tape and cut the wire to the desired length. Arrange the flowers; add a few dried leaves, if desired.

Changes in the atmosphere affect dried flowers. They keep best during winter months, and survive summer when in air-conditioned surroundings. To help them withstand the changes in weather and humidity, spray the flowers with vinyl sealant. Periodically spray the flowers with a light coating of sealant to freshen and restore their colors.

Copper Crafts for Christmas

The gleaming warmth of copper tooling foil makes it especially suitable for holiday trims. And metallic foil is simple to cut and shape. Here are an angel, tree ornaments, and a Nativity scene to bring the spirit of Christmas to life at your house.

A little time and just a few tools are all you need to transform copper foil into festive trims. Cut the foil with old scissors and add the detail lines with a pencil or dry ballpoint pen.

The Nativity figures at *right* stand on bases made from wood scraps. Let the Nativity figures help you share the Christmas story with your family and friends.

Embellish the copper angel and copper ornaments, *left*, by punching holes with a hammer and nails to create the detail lines.

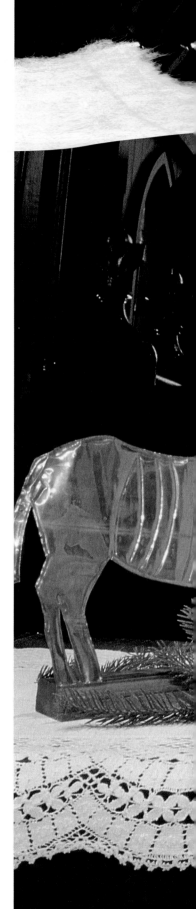

Copper Punch Ornaments

Shown on page 102.
Ornaments are 3 inches square.

MATERIALS

For each ornament

3½-inch square of copper tooling foil

Masking tape; tracing paper

Old newspapers

Scrap of plywood or board at least 8x8 inches

Ice pick or small awl

Hammer; work gloves

Steel wool; paper towels

Clear acrylic spray

Crafts glue; old scissors

3-inch square *each* of poster board and felt

½ yard of ¼-inch-wide ribbon

INSTRUCTIONS

Note: The edges of the foil may be sharp. Wear gloves to protect your hands when working with the foil.

Trace one of the patterns, *right* and *opposite,* onto tracing paper. For padding, tape folded newspapers on scrap board; tape a copper square atop newspapers. Tape the traced pattern to the foil square.

Using an ice pick or an awl, hammer evenly spaced holes, approximately ⅛ inch apart, along all of the lines. Remove the tracing paper.

Rub the surface with steel wool and buff with a paper towel. Spray the square with clear acrylic; let dry. Remove the copper square from the newspaper.

To assemble the ornament, center and glue a cardboard square to the back of the punched square and let dry. Trim the foil corners diagonally at the outer corners of the cardboard. Fold the edges of the foil to the back over the cardboard.

Glue a 6-inch-long piece of ribbon in a loop to the top corner of the cardboard back. Glue a felt square to the ornament back. Tie a 12-inch-long ribbon in a bow; glue to the top corner of the ornament.

Copper Angel

Shown on page 102.
Finished angel is 7½ inches tall.

MATERIALS

12x14-inch piece of 36-gauge copper tooling foil

12x14-inch piece of red felt

Awl or ice pick

Hammer

Tracing paper

Dry ballpoint pen

Newspapers

Steel wool

Old scissors or tin snips

Paper towels

Crafts glue

10x12-inch board, ½ to 1 inch thick, for a punching surface

Masking tape

Clothespins

Clear acrylic spray

Work gloves

INSTRUCTIONS

Note: The edges of the foil may be sharp. Wear gloves to protect your hands when working with the foil.

Trace the patterns *opposite* onto tracing paper; complete the wings and body by flopping the patterns along the center lines. Pad the board to be used as a punching surface with a layer of newspapers.

For the body, cut an 8½x12-inch piece of foil; tape it onto the newspaper pad. Tape the angel body pattern onto the foil.

Pressing very hard with a dry ballpoint pen, trace the black lines on the pattern. Using an awl or ice pick and a hammer, punch holes along the blue pattern lines. Space the holes about ⅛ inch apart. Punch holes for eyes.

Remove the pattern. Cut out the angel. Cut into the angel along the lower edges of the arms.

Rub the surface with steel wool and buff with a paper towel. Spray with clear acrylic sealer on both sides and let dry.

Bend the arms forward until the hands touch; bend the hands back slightly at the wrists. Glue the hands together. Using a clothespin padded

with a scrap of felt, clamp the hands together until the glue is dry.

Glue the angel onto an 8½x12-inch piece of felt and let dry. Trim the felt, leaving a ⅛-inch margin around the angel.

Gently roll the body into a cone, overlapping back edges of the skirt ½ inch, and glue. Using clothespins padded with felt scraps, clamp the skirt together at the top and bottom; let dry. Bend head forward slightly at the neck.

For the wings, cut a 5x6-inch piece of foil; tape it onto the newspaper pad. Pressing very hard with a dry ballpoint pen, trace the black pattern lines.

Using an awl or ice pick and a hammer, punch holes along the blue pattern lines. Space the holes about ⅛ inch apart.

Remove the pattern. Cut out the wings. Glue the wings onto a 5x6-inch piece of felt and let dry. Trim the felt, leaving a ⅛-inch margin around the wings.

Glue the wings to the angel back, placing the top notch on the wings behind the face and tucking the bottom notch inside the skirt. Using a clothespin padded with a felt scrap, clamp the top wing notch to the head; let dry.

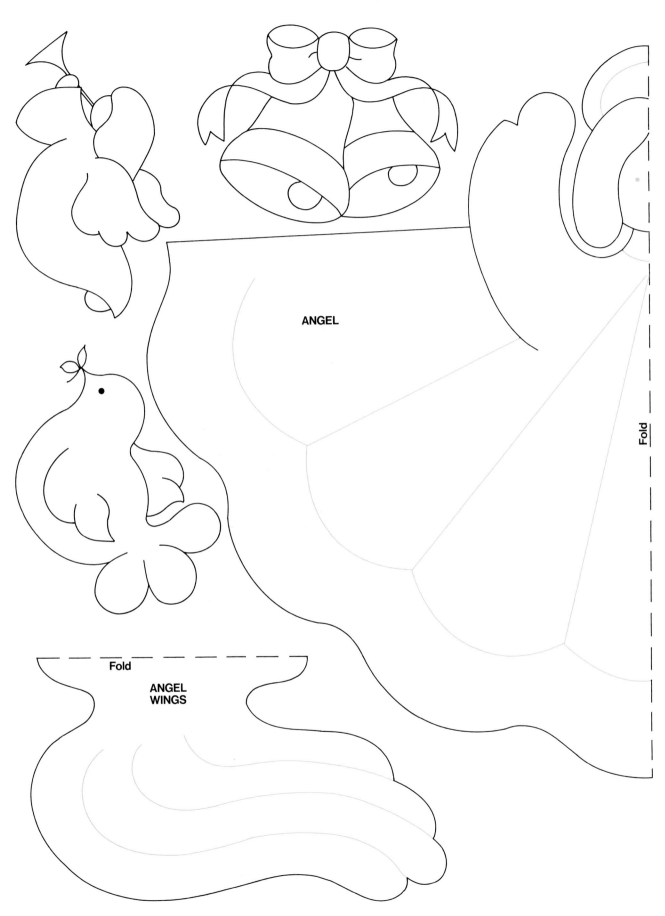

ANGEL

Fold

ANGEL
WINGS

Fold

Copper Crèche

Shown on pages 102 and 103.
Finished figures range from 5½ to
11½ inches tall.

MATERIALS

15x25-inch piece of copper tooling
    foil
15x25-inch piece of felt
Orange stick or cuticle stick to
    depress the foil
Pencil or dry ballpoint pen
Old scissors or tin snips
Tracing paper; masking tape
Steel wool; paper towels
Clear acrylic spray
1x1½x30-inch pine board
¼-inch-diameter wood dowel
Wood glue; wood stain
Work gloves; router
Drill

INSTRUCTIONS

**Note: The edges of the foil may be
sharp. When handling the foil, wear
gloves to protect your hands.**

Trace patterns, *below* and on
pages 107–109, onto tracing paper.
Tape patterns onto copper sheet.
Place felt under copper for padding.

With a pencil or a dry ballpoint
pen, trace the design lines firmly
enough to indent the copper. When
all lines have been tooled and trans-
ferred to the copper, remove the patterns. Redraw over all the lines to
define them more clearly.

Working from the front, use a cuticle or orange stick to flatten all
dark areas on the patterns. Cut out
the figures just outside the outline.

Rub the surface of each figure
with steel wool and buff with a paper towel. Spray both sides with
clear acrylic; let dry.

To make easels to support figures,
cut bases from pine board the width
of each figure. Rout ½-inch-deep
grooves ½ inch from the front edges
of easel bases. Stand figures in the
grooves to mark holes for dowels,
placing a dowel behind each leg.
Cut dowels to the height of each figure; drill holes to accept the dowels.
Stain the bases and the dowels.
Glue the dowels in the holes.

Match Line AB

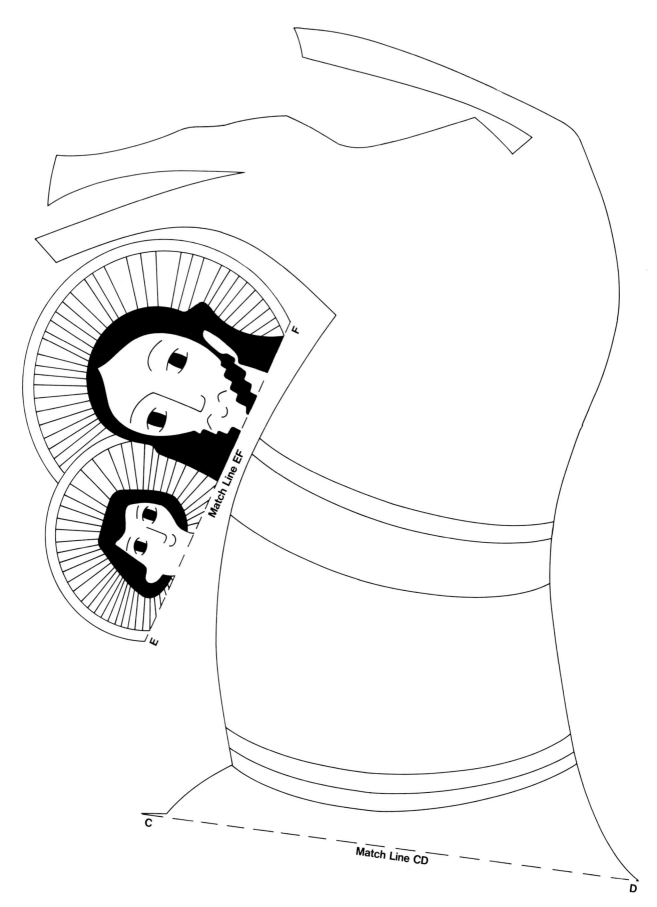

Bread-Dough Angels

With a batch of salt dough you can craft a heavenly host of adorable angels. Give each cherub a personality of its own by fashioning lambs, bears, a basket of evergreens, or armloads of stars for the angels to carry, then paint the ornaments in a variety of acrylic colors. Turn the page for how-to instructions.

Bread-Dough Angels

Shown on pages 110 and 111. Finished angels are approximately 3x5 inches.

MATERIALS
1 cup of flour
¼ cup of salt
6 tablespoons of water
Garlic press
Aluminum foil
Cookie sheet
Plastic bags
No. 20 gold craft wire
Acrylic paints
Artist's brushes
Fine-tipped permanent marker
High-gloss polyurethane
Powdered tempera paint or food
   coloring (optional)

INSTRUCTIONS
To make the dough
Place the flour and salt in a bowl. Blend about 6 tablespoons of water into the dry ingredients. The consistency of the dough should be soft but not sticky. Add extra water or flour as needed. Knead the dough until all of the salt is worked in; the dough should feel smooth.

If you decide to make several batches of dough, add powdered tempera paint or food coloring to each batch before shaping the angels. This will cut down on the painting time. Store clay in plastic bags until you are ready to use it.

Cover a cookie sheet with foil and work directly on the foil. Refer to the photograph on pages 110–111. Note: Moisten the dough with water between all joints as you add pieces to the ornament.

To make the angel
DRESS: Pinch off a piece of dough about the size of a golf ball. Press the dough between your fingers to flatten it into a ½-inch-thick dress shape. The dress should measure about 3 inches long and 4 inches wide. Pinch and fold the dough to create the dress waist, gathering it to a width of 1 inch.

SLEEVES: Roll two ½-inch-thick pieces of dough about 1½ inches long. Bend and attach the sleeves to the dress.

Pinch off a small piece of dough for the neck ruffle. Flatten dough into a thin strip that measures ½x1½ inches. Pinch one long side to gather the ruffle, and fasten it over the dress and arms.

HEAD: Roll a piece of dough into a ½-inch-thick flattened oval that measures ¾x1 inch. Attach the head to the neck ruffle.

Place a tiny piece of dough at the center of the head for the nose.

FEET: Attach ½x¾-inch feet to the center of the dress hem. Add three ⅛-inch-diameter toes to each foot.

WINGS: Shape two ½-inch-thick triangles from dough that measure 1 inch wide at the base and are 1½ inches long. Attach the wings to the angel's shoulder, layering one wing over the other.

HAIR: Push dough through a garlic press to create the hair. Style the hair as shown in the photograph on pages 110–111.

HALO: Wind gold wire around a thick pen to shape a circle. Clip the ends, leaving ½-inch ends. Twist the wire ends, and insert them into the top of the angel's head.

HANDS: Form two ⅜-inch-thick balls. Flatten them slightly, and cut four slits with a paring knife to form fingers and thumbs.

Make an armload figure as instructed below. Attach the hands to the angel around the armload figure.

To make the armload figures
TEDDY: Roll a ½-inch ball of dough for the tummy; add ¼x½-inch legs at the bottom of the tummy.

For the head, attach a slightly flattened ¼-inch ball to the top of the tummy. Add flattened pieces of dough to make the ears and muzzle.

Attach the bear between the angel's sleeves.

Add ⅛x¾-inch arms *after* the angel's hands are in place, so bear's arms hang over angel's arms.

SHEEP: Push dough through a garlic press to form a ½-inch-thick "fleece" for the body. The body should be 1 inch in diameter.

Attach four legs, each measuring ¼x¾ inch, to the body bottom.

Roll a ⅜-inch-diameter ball of dough for the head. Attach it to the upper body. Add ¼-inch ears and "fleece" to the top of the head.

Place the sheep between the angel's sleeves.

STARS: Cut stars from ⅛-inch-thick rolled dough with miniature cookie cutters, or cut out stars with a paring knife. Attach four or five stars to the angel's dress between the sleeves. Add a few more stars after the angel's hands have been attached. (See photograph for placement.)

BASKET: Roll a flattened shape for the basket bottom. It should measure 1 inch wide at the basket top and ½ inch deep. Attach to the angel's dress front.

Fill the basket with greens. To form the greens, push dough through a garlic press.

Add a ⅛-inch-thick handle over the greens and the angel's sleeve.

To finish the angel
Bake the ornaments at 275° about 3 hours. Check the ornaments periodically during baking to avoid burning or overdrying them. Ornaments are done when they are hard.

Allow ornaments to cool completely before painting.

Using artist's paintbrushes, paint the ornaments with acrylic paints, using the photograph on pages 110–111 for color ideas.

Draw on the eyes and animal mouths with a fine-tip marker.

Coat the painted ornaments with high-gloss polyurethane.

Safety Tips for a Happy Holiday Season

As enchanting as it is, your family's beautiful evergreen with its twinkling lights and glittering decorations can be a safety hazard. Take these precautions to guard against fire and other accidents in your home during the holiday season.

CHOOSING A TREE: If you buy an artificial Christmas tree, make sure it's been tested for flammability by Underwriters Laboratories and bears their seal of approval.

If you opt for a real tree, choose a fresh one. Fresh trees have a high moisture content; they are less likely to dry out and catch fire. If the needles are brown and break off easily, the tree is a greater fire risk.

Test the needles by flexing them between your thumb and forefinger. The needles should bend but not break. Next, lift the tree a few inches off the ground, then drop it on its base. Only a few needles should fall.

Store a fresh tree outdoors in a bucket of water, away from the sun and wind, until you're ready to bring it indoors and decorate it. Mist the tree occasionally to keep the branches moist.

SETTING UP A TREE: Just before you bring the tree inside, cut an inch or two off the bottom of the trunk so the tree can take in water easily.

Clean the tree stand with a small amount of household bleach mixed with water before you use it. The bleach kills microorganisms that can reduce the tree's water intake.

Place the tree in a location away from the fireplace, radiator, and other heat sources. Avoid placing the tree where it interferes with the traffic pattern in your home, and see that it doesn't block a doorway.

When you have selected the location for the tree, place a plastic drop cloth under the tree stand to protect the floor.

All through the holiday season, keep the tree moist. Fill the tree stand with enough lukewarm water to cover the cut end of the trunk, and keep it at that level. Check the amount of water in the stand daily; a tree can consume as much as a gallon of water a day.

DECORATING A TREE: **Never use lighted candles on a tree or near evergreens or draperies.** Instead, use electric lights that have been checked for safety. (Look for the Underwriters Laboratories [UL] seal.)

Check each light set for broken or cracked sockets, frayed or bare wires, and loose connections. Repair or discard faulty light strings.

Replace any burned-out lamps on electrical decorations only with the lamps specified on the package.

Use only manufacturer's specified fuses to replace burned-out fuses on light strings. Never use aluminum foil or differently rated fuses to replace burned-out fuses.

Keep light strings, decorative lamps, and other electrical decorations out of the reach of small children.

Fasten lights securely to the tree. If possible, avoid letting the bulbs touch the needles or branches.

Don't put more than three sets of lights on a single extension cord. Don't use more than one extension cord.

Keep electrical cords away from the tree's water supply.

Never use decorative light strings marked "For Indoor Use" on trees outdoors.

To prevent electrical shock, do not use electrical decorations on trees with metallic needles, leaves, or branches. Instead, use color spotlights above or beside a metallic tree.

Use decorations that are noncombustible or flame-resistant.

Use lead-free tinsel.

Hang breakable ornaments on the upper branches of the tree, out of the reach of small children.

DISPOSING OF A TREE: If you've used a plastic drop cloth under the tree, after the holidays fold the drop cloth around the tree to catch needles and branches that may break off as you carry the tree outdoors.

Plastic bags, large enough to hold a Christmas tree, are available in the tree-trimming departments at many stores. The large bags make tree removal easy.

Burning evergreens in a fireplace is dangerous; flames can flare out and send sparks flying about the room. Give your tree to the garbage collector.

Equip your home with a UL-listed ABC-type fire extinguisher and smoke or heat detectors.

Always turn off the tree lights before leaving the house or going to bed.

Needlepoint Symbols of the Season

You won't need to follow a chart to stitch these whimsical Christmas ornaments. Thanks to the full-size patterns on pages 115–119, these trims are as easy as filling in a child's coloring book.

Needlepoint Ornaments

Shown on pages 114 and 115. Ornaments range from 4 to 7 inches long.

MATERIALS

For each ornament

8-inch square of both 10-count needlepoint canvas and felt
Assorted colors of three-ply Paternayan yarn
Masking tape; monofilament
Permanent felt-tip pen; crafts glue
1 to 1½ yards of gold trim

INSTRUCTIONS

Select one of the patterns *below* or on pages 117–119.

Center the piece of needlepoint canvas over the pattern. Secure the canvas to the pattern with masking tape so the canvas won't slip. Trace the pattern lines onto the canvas with a felt-tip pen.

Using the continental or basket-weave stitch and two strands of Paternayan yarn, stitch over all the pattern lines in a dark yarn to outline the design. Then, fill in the outlined areas with colored yarns.

After the stitching is complete, return the canvas to its original shape by blocking. Using a damp press-cloth, steam-press the canvas from the back side. If pressing doesn't straighten the canvas, dampen the yarn and stretch it into shape by tacking the canvas to a board with rustproof tacks.

Cut out ornaments ⅛ inch from edges. Glue ornaments to felt for a backing. Trim felt to the shape of the ornament, leaving a ⅛-inch border of felt around ornament.

Glue gold trim over the raw canvas edges. Tie trim in a bow and glue to the top of the ornament.

Thread a needle with monofilament, and run the monofilament through the ornament top. Tie it into a hanging loop.

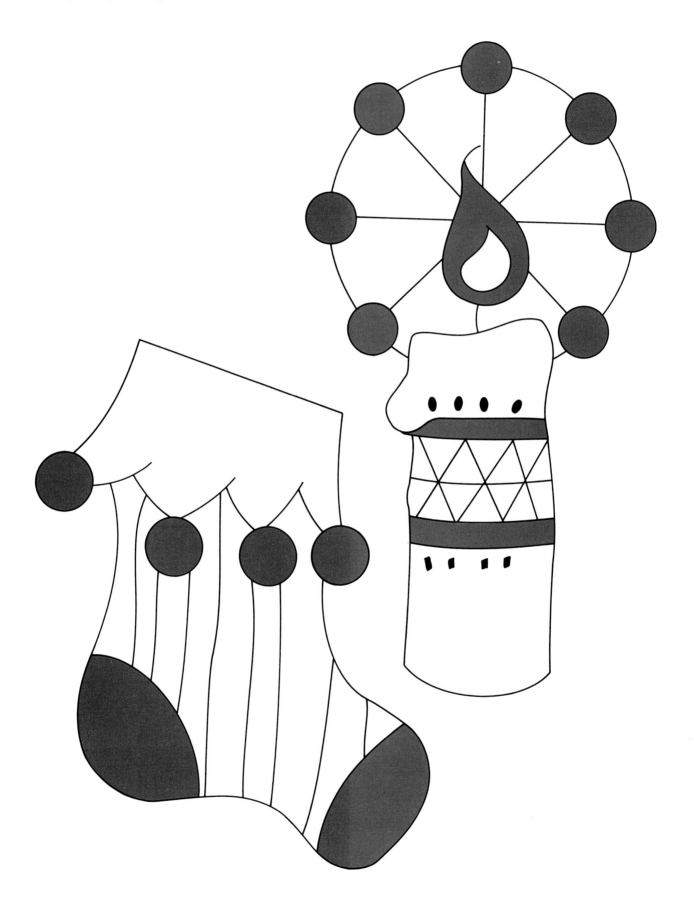

Festive Crochet

Romantic and elegant, crocheted trims and accessories are just what you need to add sparkle to your Christmas decor. Snowflakes, in white or pastels, look as crisp as ice crystals on the tree. A star-spangled cloth dresses up the simplest of party tables. And place mats worked in the pineapple pattern extend a lively symbolic welcome to guests.

Because it is made in blocks, the 40-inch-square tablecloth at *right* is easy to adapt to any table size. Add more 6-inch blocks to increase the size of the tablecloth or use fewer blocks to make it smaller.

The lacy crocheted snowflakes, *left,* are quick to make. Each of the three 2¾- to 4-inch designs is created in only two or three rounds. Vary the colors and thread sizes to add variety to your tree. Because they are fast and easy to work, you'll want to make extras as gifts.

Welcome guests to your holiday table for morning coffee or evening dessert with crocheted pineapple place mats. The pineapple, a traditional American symbol of hospitality, is a favorite choice for crocheted tablecloths, doilies, place mats, or any item that might be used for special occasions or elegant entertaining.

The beautifully detailed place mats, *opposite,* are a stunning example of classic pineapple-crochet style. The open design of these 14x17½-inch oval place mats allows the color of your cloth or the luster of a finely polished wooden tabletop to show.

The 11x17-inch natural-colored linen place mat, *right,* is trimmed with pineapple edging worked with firm white thread. Worked directly in the hem, the edging is easily adjusted to any size place mat or tablecloth.

Directions for the table linens and lacy crocheted snowflake ornaments begin on page 124.

Christmas Star Tablecloth

Shown on page 120 and 121. Tablecloth is approximately 40 inches square; finished block is 6 inches square before joining (see Note below).

MATERIALS

9 balls of white J. & P. Coats Knit-Cro-Sheen crochet cotton
No. 7 steel crochet hook
Sewing thread

Abbreviations: See page 128.
Gauge: In rows of double crochet, 9 dc = 1 inch, 4 rows = 1 inch

INSTRUCTIONS

Note: A finished block is 6 inches square before joining. Blocks made of cotton thread will be about 5 inches across after hot water washing, so allow for shrinkage when figuring the desired size for the tablecloth.

The tablecloth shown in the photograph is made of 64 blocks sewn together in eight rows with eight blocks in each row. Adjust the size of the tablecloth by making more or fewer blocks.

BLOCK MOTIF (Make 64): Ch 8, join with sl st to form ring.

Rnd 1: Ch 3, 23 dc in ring, join with sl st to top of ch-3.

Rnd 2: Ch 3, 2 dc in next dc, dc in next dc, (ch 1, dc in next dc, 2 dc in next dc, dc in next dc) 7 times; end ch 1, join with sl st to top of ch-3.

Rnd 3: Ch 3, (2 dc in next dc) twice, dc in next dc; (ch 2, dc in next dc, 2 dc in next 2 dc, dc in next dc) 7 times, ch 2; join to top of ch-3.

Rnd 4: Ch 3, * 2 dc in next dc, dc in next 2 dc, 2 dc in next dc, dc in next dc, ch 2; dc in first dc of next group. Rep from * around; join to top of ch-3.

Rnds 5 and 6: Work same as Rnd 4, having 2 more dc in each group on each row—12 dc in each section on Rnd 6.

Rnd 7: Ch 2, dc in next dc; * dc in next 8 dc; holding back on hook last lp of each st, dc in each of last 2 dc, yo, draw through all lps on hook—dc-dec made. Ch 3, work dc-dec in first 2 dc of next grp, dc in next 8 dc, work dc-dec in last 2 dc of grp, ch 2, make trc, ch 3, trc in next ch-2 sp—corner made. Ch 2, work dc-dec in first 2 dc on next grp; rep from * around; end corner in last ch-2 sp, ch 2; join to top of first dc.

Rnd 8: Ch 2, dc in next dc; * dc in next 6 dc, work dc-dec in last 2 dc, ch 3, dc in ch-3 sp, ch 3, dc-dec in first 2 dc of next grp, dc in each of next 6 dc, dc-dec in last 2 dc of grp, ch 3, trc in trc, ch 3, corner in ch-3 sp, ch 3, trc in next trc, ch 3; dc-dec in first 2 dc of next grp; rep from * around; end ch 3, join to the top of the first dc.

Rnd 9: Ch 2, dc in next dc; * dc in next 4 dc, work dc-dec in last 2 dc, ch 2, dc in next ch-3 sp, ch 2, dc in dc, ch 2, dc in next ch-3 sp, ch 2; dc-dec in first 2 dc of next group, dc in next 4 dc, dc-dec in last 2 dc of grp, (ch 3, trc in next trc) twice, ch 3; holding back on hook last lp of each st, work 3 trc in ch-3 corner sp, yo, draw through all lps on hook—trc-cl made; ch 3, trc-cl in same sp; (ch 3, trc in next trc) twice, ch 3, dc-dec in first 2 dc of next grp; rep from * around; end ch 3, join to top of first dc made.

Rnd 10: Ch 2, dc in next dc; * dc in next 2 dc, work dc-dec in last 2 dc, (ch 3, dc in next dc) 3 times, ch 3; dc-dec in first 2 dc of next grp, dc in next 2 dc, dc-dec in last 2 dc of grp; (ch 3, trc in next trc) twice, ch 3, trc-cl in next sp, ch 3; work trc-cl, ch 3, trc-cl in corner sp; ch 3, trc-cl in next sp; (ch 3, trc in next trc) twice, ch 3, work dc-dec in first 2 dc of next grp.

Rep from * around; end with ch 3. Join to top of first dc made.

Rnd 11: Ch 2; holding back on hook last lp of each st, make dc in each of next 3 dc, thread over, and draw through all lps on hook—beg cl made; * ch 2, dc in next sp, (ch 1, dc in dc, ch 1, dc in next sp) 3 times, ch 2, make dc-cl over next 4 dc, ch 3, dc in next trc, ch 3, sc in next sp, (ch 5, sc in next space) 3 times, ch 6, sc in same corner sp (ch 5, sc in next sp) 3 times; ch 3, dc in next dc, ch 3, make dc-cl over 4 dc; rep from * around; end ch 3, join to top of first cl made. Fasten off.

ASSEMBLY: With sewing thread, sew the edges of the two motifs together using overcast stitches.

First, overcast the dc-cls and dcs on the side edges of two motifs together. Then overcast the center of the ch-5 lps and the tip of the corner lps together.

Assemble the motifs into eight strips with eight motifs in each strip. Then sew the strips together.

FINISHING: After the blocks are sewn together, join thread in any corner lp, ch 1, work 8 sc in same lp; work scs in ch-lps across side edges, spacing to keep the work lying flat and working the same number of sc in each corresponding size lp. Work 8 sc in each corner lp; join to first sc.

Crocheted Snowflakes

Shown on pages 120 and 121. White snowflakes are approximately 3½ to 4 inches in diameter; pastel snowflakes are approximately 2¾ to 3 inches in diameter.

MATERIALS

DMC's Cébélia white cotton crochet thread, Size 10
Size 10 steel crochet hook (for white snowflakes)
DMC Cébélia crochet cotton, Size 20: light green, No. 955; peach, No. 754; pink, No. 818; and lavender, No. 210
Size 12 steel crochet hook (for pastel snowflakes)
White crafts glue; paper towels
Sponge brush
Rustproof pins
Monofilament line

Snowflake No. 1

Snowflake No. 2

Snowflake No. 3

INSTRUCTIONS
Snowflake No. 1

Starting at the center, ch 7, join with sl st to form a ring.

Rnd 1: Ch 3, 2 dc in ring, * ch 3, 3 dc in ring; repeat from * 4 more times; end ch 3, join with sl st to top of ch-3 at the beginning of the round.

Rnd 2: Ch 1, * sc in same st as join and next 2 dc; 2 sc in ch-3 sp, ch 9, sl st in the ninth chain from hook—stem made, ch 10, sl st in ninth chain from hook, ch 3, (ch 2, hdc in second chain from hook, ch 2, sl st in same st as hdc—picot made) 5 times; sl st in base chain of first picot to form a circle; sl st in next 3 chains below the picots; ch 9, sl st in ninth chain from hook, sl st in base chain of the opposite stem, sl st in next chain, ch 9, sl st in ninth chain from hook, sl st in base chain of opposite stem; 2 sc in same ch-3 sp; repeat from * 5 more times, working sc in 3 dc at beginning of each repeat hereafter; join with sl st to sc at beginning of round. Fasten off.

Snowflake No. 2

Starting at the center, ch 7, join with sl st to form a ring.

Rnd 1: (Ch 4, 2 trc in ring, ch 4, sl st in ring) 6 times.

Rnd 2: Sl st in next 4 ch; ch 4, retaining last loop of each trc on hook, trc in next 2 trc and top of ch-4, yo, draw through all 4 lps on hook, ch 1—beginning cluster made; * ch 6, sl st in fifth ch from hook. Let work dangle from the loop on the hook and twirl naturally so that you can work from right to left in the loop; ch 4, in ch-5 lp work the following: trc, ch 3, sc, (ch 3, trc, ch 3, sc) twice, ch 3, trc, ch 4, and sl st; sl st in ch above cluster, sl st in top of cluster, ch 9; retaining last lp of each trc on hook, trc in top of next ch-4, next 2 trc, and top of next ch-4; yo, draw through all 5 lps on hook, ch 1—cluster made.

Repeat from * 5 more times.

End ch 9, join with sl st to top of first cluster.

Fasten off.

Snowflake No. 3

Starting at the center, ch 7, join with sl st to form a ring.

Rnd 1: Ch 3, work 2 dc in ring, * ch 3, work 3 dc in ring; repeat from * 4 more times; end ch 3, join rnd with sl st in top of ch-3—six 3-dc groups made.

Rnd 2: Sl st in next 2 dc and ch-3 space; ch 3, in same space work 2 dc, ch 10, 3 dc; * ch 1, in next ch-3 space work 3 dc, ch 10, 3 dc; repeat from * 4 more times; end ch 1, join with sl st to top of ch-3 at beginning of the round.

Rnd 3: Work the following in each ch-10 loop around: 3 dc, ch 2, sc, ch 2, 2 dc, ch 2, sc, (ch 2, dc, ch 1, ch 2, hdc in second ch from hook, ch 2, sl st in same ch as hdc—picot made. Work another picot, sl st in ch-1 be-low picots, dc, ch 2, sc) twice, ch 2, 2 dc, ch 2, sc, ch 2, and 3 dc. Sl st in next ch-1 sp. Fasten off.

Blocking instructions

If necessary, wash the ornaments in warm water and mild detergent. Rinse thoroughly. Wrap the snowflakes in a towel and squeeze out the excess moisture.

Place two or three layers of paper towels on top of a padded board.

Pin a snowflake to the board as follows: Place a pin in the top of each cluster, then pin the other detail picots.

Dry the snowflakes away from heat and light.

Dilute the crafts glue with water into a mixture that is two-thirds glue and one-third water.

Place dried and blocked snowflakes on waxed paper. Use the sponge brush to saturate them with the glue mixture. Carefully pick up each snowflake and place it on a fresh piece of waxed paper. Allow to dry.

Cut an 8- to 10-inch piece of monofilament line for each ornament. Thread a monofilament piece through the top of each snowflake; tie to make hanging loops. Suspend the ornaments on the tree.

To enjoy your snowflakes beyond Christmas and throughout the winter, suspend them in a window with clear rubber suction cups such as those used to hang stained glass.

Crocheted Pineapple Place Mats

Shown on page 122.
Oval mats are approximately 14x17½ inches.

MATERIALS
For four place mats
J. & P. Coats Big Ball Best 6-Cord Mercerized Cotton, Size 30: 7 balls (350 yards each) of No. 1 white
No. 10 steel crochet hook

INSTRUCTIONS
MOTIF (make 2): *Rnd 1:* Starting at the center, ch 12. Join with sl st to form ring.

Rnd 1: Ch 3, 23 dc in ring. Join to top of ch-3.

Rnd 2: Ch 4, * dc in next dc, ch 1. Rep from * around. Join to third ch of ch-4.

Rnd 3: Ch 1, sc in first sp, * ch 5, sc in next sp. Rep from * around. End with ch 2, dc in first sc to form last lp—24 loops made.

Rnds 4 and 5: Ch 1, sc in lp just formed, * ch 5, sc in next lp. Rep from * around, end with ch 2, dc in first sc.

Rnd 6: Ch 1, sc in lp just formed, * ch 6, sc in next lp. Rep from * around, end with ch 3, dc in first sc.

Rnd 7: Ch 1, sc in lp just formed, * ch 7, sc in next lp. Rep from * around, end with ch 3, tr in first sc. Fasten off.

FIRST PINEAPPLE: With the right side of the motif facing you, join thread to any loop on the last rnd of a motif.

Row 1: Ch 3, in same lp make dc, ch 2, and 2 dc—starting shell made.

Ch 1; in next lp on motif make 2 dc, ch 5, and 2 dc; ch 1; in next lp on motif make 2 dc, ch 2, and 2 dc—shell made.

Ch 5, turn.

Row 2: Make shell in sp of next shell—shell over shell made.

Ch 1, 15 tr in next ch-5 sp, ch 1, shell over shell. Ch 5, turn.

Row 3: Shell over shell, ch 1, (tr in next tr, ch 1) 14 times; tr in next tr, ch 1, shell over shell. Ch 5, turn.

Row 4: Shell over shell, ch 4, skip next ch-1 sp, sc in next ch-1 sp, (ch 3, sc in next sp) 13 times; ch 4, shell over shell. Ch 5, turn.

Rows 5–15: Shell over shell, ch 4, sc in next ch-3 lp, * ch 3, sc in next ch-3 lp.

Rep from * to next ch-4 sp, ch 4, shell over shell. Ch 5, turn.

Row 16: Shell over shell, ch 4, sc in next ch-3 lp, ch 3, sc in next lp, ch 4, shell over shell. Ch 5, turn.

Row 17: Shell over shell, ch 4, sc in ch-3 lp, ch 4, 2 dc in sp of next shell, ch 1, sl st in sp of last shell made, ch 1, 2 dc in same sp where last 2 dc were made. Ch 5, turn. Sl st in sp of previous shell. Fasten off.

SECOND PINEAPPLE: * With the right side of the same motif facing you, skip 1 lp on last rnd of motif following last pineapple. Join thread to next lp on motif.

Starting with Row 1, work same as for the previous pineapple *.

THIRD, FOURTH PINEAPPLES: Follow the instructions from * to * of Second Pineapple.

SECOND MOTIF: Work four pineapples on the second motif in the same way.

With the points of the pineapples toward the outer edge, place the motifs side by side on a flat surface.

Sew the center free lp of each motif to the corresponding lp on the other motif.

EDGING: With the right side of a motif facing and the four pineapples attached, and counting up from the base of the fourth pineapple, join thread to fourth ch-5, turning chain lp along its left edge.

Rnd 1: Ch 1, sc in same lp, ch 5, * sc in third ch-5 turning lp from base of next pineapple, (ch 7, sc in next ch-5 turning lp) 11 times; ch 5.

Rep from * around, end last rep with (ch 7, sc in next ch-5 turning lp) 10 times; ch 3, tr in first sc to form last lp.

Rnd 2: Ch 2, sc in next ch-7 lp, * (ch 8, sc in next lp) 10 times; ch 2, skip next ch-5 lp, sc in next lp. Rep from * around, end last rep with (ch 8, sc in next lp) 9 times; ch 4, tr in tr.

Rnd 3: Ch 1, sc in next ch-8 lp, (ch 9, sc in next lp) 9 times; * sc in next ch-8 lp, ch 4, sl st in last ch-9 lp made, ch 4, sc in next ch-8 lp, (ch 9, sc in next lp) 8 times. Rep from * around, end last rep with (ch 9, sc in next lp) 7 times; ch 5, dtr in tr. Join with sl st in first ch-9 lp. Fasten off.

Rnd 4: Join thread to next free ch-9 lp, ch 1, sc in same lp, * (ch 10, sc in next lp) twice; ch 10; holding back on hook the last lp of each tr, make 3 tr in next lp, thread over, and draw through all lps on hook—cluster made; (ch 10, cluster in same lp) twice; (ch 10, sc in next lp) 3 times, ch 10, skip next 2 joined lps, sc in next free ch-9 lp. Rep from * around, omitting the sc at end of last rep. Join.

Rnd 5: Sl st to center of next lp, ch 1, sc in same lp, * (ch 10, sc in next lp) 34 times; (ch 5, sc in next lp) twice. Rep from * once more, omitting the sc at end of rep. Join.

Rnd 6: Sl st to center of next lp, ch 1, sc in same lp, * (ch 10, sc in next lp) 7 times; ** ch 7, sc in next lp, (ch 10, sc in next lp) 8 times. Rep from ** once more; ch 7, sc in next lp, (ch 10, sc in next lp) 7 times; ch 8, skip next 2 ch-5 lps, sc in next lp. Rep from * once more, omitting the sc at end of rep. Join.

Rnd 7: Sl st to center of next lp, ch 1, sc in same lp, * (ch 13, sc in next lp) 6 times; **ch 11, skip next lp, sc in next lp, (ch 13, sc in next lp) 7 times. Rep from ** once more; ch 11, skip next lp, sc in next lp, (ch 13, sc in next lp) 6 times; ch 9, skip next lp, sc in next lp. Rep from * once more, omitting the sc at end of rep. Join. Fasten off.

FILL-IN MOTIF: Starting at the center, ch 10. Join to form ring.

Rnd 1: Ch 1, sc in ring, (ch 5, sc in ring) 11 times; ch 2, dc in first sc.

Rnd 2: (Ch 5, sc in next lp) 11 times; ch 2, dc in the dc.

Rnd 3: Ch 2, sl st in second free lp on motif, ch 2, sc in next lp on Fill-In Motif, ch 2, sc in next lp on motif, ch 2, sc in next lp on Fill-In Motif, ch 5, sc in next lp on motif, ch 2, sl st in second free lp on next motif, ch 2, sc in next lp on Fill-In Motif, ch 2, sc in next lp on same motif, ch 2, sc in next lp on Fill-In Motif, ch 5, sc in next lp on Fill-In Motif; then continue as before, joining lps of Fill-In Motif to corresponding ch-5, turning lps on next 2 adjacent pineapples, end with ch 5, sl st in dc. Fasten off.

Work the other Fill-In Motif in the same way.

Starch lightly and block to the measurements given.

Crocheted Pineapple Edging on Linen Place Mat

Shown on page 123.
Finished place mat with the edging added is 15x21 inches.

MATERIALS
11½x17½-inch piece of natural-colored linen fabric
1 Big Ball Clark's white crochet cotton, Size 30
Size 11 steel crochet hook

INSTRUCTIONS
FABRIC PREPARATION: Pull fabric threads to use as cutting guidelines. Trim the linen so it is an 11½x17½-inch rectangle. Turn the outer edges under ¼ inch so the linen measures 11x17 inches. Press; machine-stitch the hem.

EDGING: *Rnd 1:* Beginning at left-hand corner of short side, put 3 scs in corner. Continue to sc evenly around piece, anchoring sts inside hemline and putting 3 scs in each corner. Work 166 sc along long sides and 95 sc along short sides. Pattern is a multiple of 7 sts and can be adjusted to fit any size cloth.

Rnd 2: Sl st into next sc, ch 7, trc in same st as sl st, (ch 3, trc in same sc as last trc) twice—beg corner made; * ch 6, sk 6 sc, dc in next sc, ch 3, dc in same st as last dc—V-st made. Rep from * until 23 V-sps made along long side; ch 6, sk 6 sc, in next sc work (trc, ch 3) 3 times, trc in same sc—corner made; rep from * across short side, working 13 V-sps along this side and working corner in center sc of 3-sc corner grp; work rem 2 sides to correspond; end ch 6, join with sl st to fourth ch of beg ch-7.

Rnd 3: Sl st into ch-3 sp, ch 3, dc in same sp, ch 2, 2 dc in same sp—beg shell made. (Ch 2, in next ch-3 sp work 2 dc, ch 2, 2 dc—shell made) twice; * (ch 5, shell in ch-3 sp of next V-st; ch 5, 8 trc in ch-3 sp of next V-st) 11 times; ch 5, shell in ch-3 sp of V-st, ch 5, (shell in next ch-3 lp, ch 2) twice, shell in next ch-3 lp; rep from * across next side, working sts between first set of ( )s 6 times. Work rem 2 sides to correspond; end ch 5, join with sl st to top of ch-3.

Rnd 4: Sl st in next dc and ch-2 sp and work a beg shell in same sp; (ch 5, shell in ch-2 sp of next shell) 3 times; * ch 5, sc bet first and second trc of 8-trc grp, (ch 3, sc bet next 2 trcs) 6 times; ch 5, shell in shell; rep from * 10 more times, (ch 5, shell in next shell) 4 times; rep from first *, working between the *s a total of 6 times instead of 10. Work rem 2 sides to correspond; end ch 5, join with sl st to top of beg ch-3.

Rnd 5: Sl st in next dc and ch-2 sp and work a beg shell in same sp; (ch 5, shell in ch-2 sp of next shell) 3 times; * ch 5, sc in next ch-3 lp, (ch 3, sc in next ch-3 lp) 5 times; ch 5, shell in shell, rep from * 10 more times, (ch 5, shell in next shell) 4 times; rep from first *, working between the *s a total of 6 times instead of 10. Work rem 2 sides to correspond; end ch 5, join with sl st to top of beg ch-3.

Rnd 6: Sl st in next dc and ch-2 sp and work a beg shell in same sp; (ch 3, shell in center ch of next ch-5 lp, ch 3, shell in next shell) twice; * ch 5, in ch-2 sp of next shell work (2 dc, ch 2) twice, 2 dc in same sp; ch 5, sc in next ch-3 lp, (ch 3, sc in next ch-3 lp) 4 times; rep from * 10 more times; ch 5, in ch-2 sp of next shell work (2 dc, ch 2) twice, 2 dc in same sp; ch 5, (shell in shell, ch 3, shell in center ch of next ch-5 lp, ch 3) twice, shell in shell; rep from first *, working bet the *s 6 times instead of 10. Work rem 2 sides to correspond; end ch 5, join with sl st to top of beg ch-3.

Rnd 7: Sl st in next dc and ch-2 sp and work a beg shell in same sp; (ch 5, shell in next shell) 5 times; ch 2, shell in shell; * ch 5, sc in next ch-3 lp, (ch 3, sc in next ch-3 lp) 3 times, ch 5, shell in shell, ch 2, shell in shell; rep from * 10 more times; (ch 5, shell in shell) 6 times; ch 2, shell in shell; rep from first *, working bet the *s 6 times instead of 10. Work rem sides to correspond; end ch 5, join to top of beg ch-3.

Rnd 8: Sl st in next dc and ch-2 sp and work a beg shell in same sp; (ch 5, shell in next shell) 6 times; * ch 5, sc in ch-3 lp, (ch 3, sc in next lp) twice; (ch 5, shell in next shell) twice; rep from * 10 more times, (ch 5, shell in next shell) 7 times; rep from first *, working bet the *s 6 times instead of 10. Work rem 2 sides to correspond; end ch 5, join to top of ch-3.

Rnd 9: Sl st in next dc and ch-2 sp and work a beg shell in same sp; (ch 10, shell in next shell) 6 times; * ch 5, sc in ch-3 lp, ch 3, sc in next ch-3 lp; ch 5, shell in shell, ch 10, shell in shell, rep from * 10 more times; (ch 10, shell in next shell) 7 times; rep from first *, working bet *s 6 times instead of 10. Work rem 2 sides to correspond; end ch 5, join to top of ch-3.

Rnd 10: Sl st in next dc and ch-2 sp, ch 1, sc in same sp; (in next ch-10 lp work 6 dc, ch 5, 6 dc; sc in ch-2 sp of next shell) 6 times; * ch 6, sc in next ch-3 lp, ch 6, sc in ch-2 sp of next shell; in next ch-10 lp work 6 dc, ch 5, 6 dc; sc in ch-2 sp of next shell; rep from * 10 more times; (in next ch-10 lp work 6 dc, ch 5, 6 dc; sc in ch-2 sp of next shell) 7 times; rep from first *, working bet *s 6 times instead of 10. Work rem 2 sides to correspond; end ch 5, join to top of ch-3. Fasten off.

BASIC CROCHET STITCHES

CROCHET ABBREVIATIONS

beg .... begin(ning)	lp(s) .... loop(s)	sk .... skip
ch .... chain	MC .... main color	sl st .... slip stitch
dc .... double crochet	pat .... pattern	sp .... space
dec .... decrease	psso .... pass slip st over	st(s) .... stitch(es)
dtr .... double treble	rem .... remaining	tog .... together
grp .... group	rep .... repeat	trc .... treble crochet
hdc .... half-double crochet	rnd .... round	yo .... yarn over
inc .... increase	sc .... single crochet	* ..... repeat from * as indicated

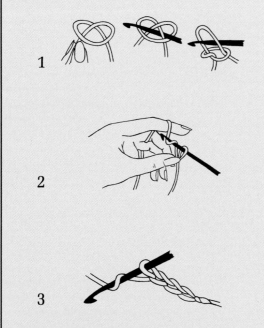

1

2

3

CHAIN STITCH

Make a slipknot on the crochet hook about 6 inches from end of yarn (1, *above*). Pull one end to tighten knot. Hold hook between right index finger and thumb, as you would a pencil. Wrap yarn over ring finger, under middle finger, and over index finger; hold short end between thumb and index finger. For more tension, wrap yarn around little finger. Insert hook under and over strand of yarn (2).

To make a foundation chain, catch the strand of yarn with the hook; draw through the loop (3). Make chain the length pattern calls for.

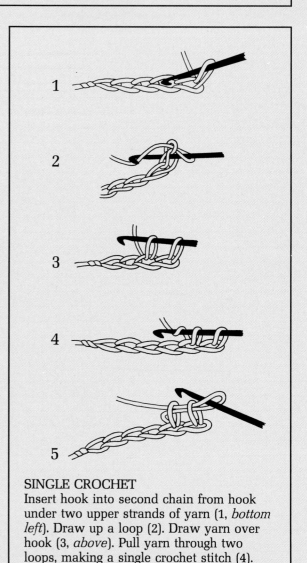

1

2

3

4

5

SINGLE CROCHET

Insert hook into second chain from hook under two upper strands of yarn (1, *bottom left*). Draw up a loop (2). Draw yarn over hook (3, *above*). Pull yarn through two loops, making a single crochet stitch (4). Insert hook into next stitch; repeat steps.

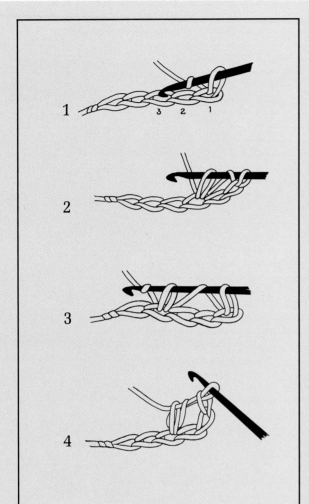

HALF–DOUBLE CROCHET
Wrap yarn over hook, insert the hook into the third chain, under two top loops (1, *above*). Draw the yarn through the chain loops (2). Wrap yarn over hook (3). Draw strand through all three loops on the hook, completing the half-double crochet (4).

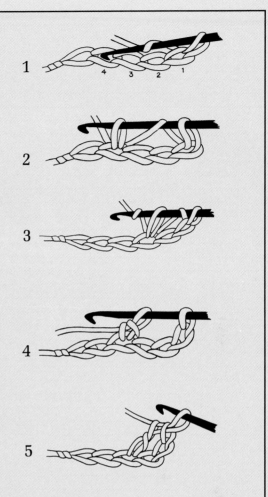

DOUBLE CROCHET
Holding yarn over hook, insert hook into fourth chain under two upper strands of yarn (1, *above*). Draw up a loop (2). Wrap yarn over hook (3). Draw yarn through two loops as shown (4). Yarn over again and draw through the last two loops on the hook (5) to complete the stitch.

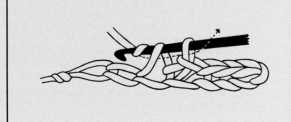

SLIP STITCH
After you have made the foundation chain, insert crochet hook under top strand of second chain from hook; yarn over. With a single motion, pull yarn through stitch and loop on hook. Insert hook under top strand of next chain, then yarn over and draw yarn through stitch and loop on the hook. Repeat this procedure to end of chain. Use this stitch for decreasing.

Special Quilts for the Holiday Season

Start a tradition at your house by stitching a quilt to use just at Christmas. Here, and on the next two pages, are pieced and appliquéd designs full of spirit and symbolism appropriate to the season.

The Country Star quilt, *right,* pieced from humble fabrics familiar to all of us—rustic red and green calicoes and simple unbleached muslin— captures the spirit of a pioneer Christmas. To give your Country Star quilt a city look, choose solid-color fabrics and sophisticated geometric prints.

This 74-inch-square bedcover is assembled from 16 large (15-inch-square) blocks. Sewn together block to block (without sashing strips), the quilt squares form both primary and secondary patterns, a star and a square bordered by half-stars.

Instructions begin on page 136.

During the mid-19th century, red, green, and white was a popular color scheme for elegant appliquéd quilts. Prized as family heirlooms and sought after by collectors, these quilts are especially appropriate to display during the Christmas season.

The 86x94-inch Pineapple and Star quilt, *left,* is made from 16 large blocks, each 19½ inches square. The blocks are arranged in four rows, with four blocks in each row.

At the center of each block is a four-point star surrounded by four pineapples topped with gracefully branching, vivid red leaves.

A narrow vine meanders along the 8-inch-wide borders on three sides of the quilt. In each curve of the vine, red pineapple tops, slightly smaller than those in the blocks, are set atop stems and green leaves to form the border flowers.

Instructions for this project begin on page 134.

Pineapple and Star Quilt

Shown on pages 132 and 133.
Finished quilt is 86x94 inches.

MATERIALS

1½ yards of red fabric
3¼ yards of green fabric for quilt top and binding
10 yards of white fabric for quilt top and back
Quilt batting
Cardboard or plastic for templates

INSTRUCTIONS

The instructions list the number of pieces to cut for the quilt, followed, in parentheses, by the number to cut for one block.

TO BEGIN: Trace patterns, *opposite*. Make cardboard or plastic templates for the patterns. The appliqué patterns are finished size. To use templates, draw around templates on the *right* side of fabric, leaving at least ½ inch between pieces. Add ¼-inch seam allowances when cutting pieces from fabric.

CUTTING INSTRUCTIONS: From the white fabric, cut two pieces, *each* 3 yards long, for the quilt back; set them aside.

From the remaining white fabric, cut two 8½x80-inch side borders and one 8½x96-inch bottom border. Cut 16 squares, *each* 20x20 inches, for the blocks. The measurements for the borders and blocks include ¼-inch seam allowances. (Finished blocks will measure 19½ inches square.) The borders will be trimmed to length when added to quilt top.

From the red fabric, cut 16 (1) of piece A and 64 (4) of piece C. Cut 25 of piece F for the borders.

From the green fabric, cut 128 (8) of piece D for the blocks and 50 of piece D for the borders. Cut 64 (4) of piece B for the blocks.

From the remaining green fabric, cut 24 yards of 1¼-inch-wide bias. Set aside 11 yards of bias for the quilt binding.

continued

PINEAPPLE STAR QUILT BLOCK PATTERN

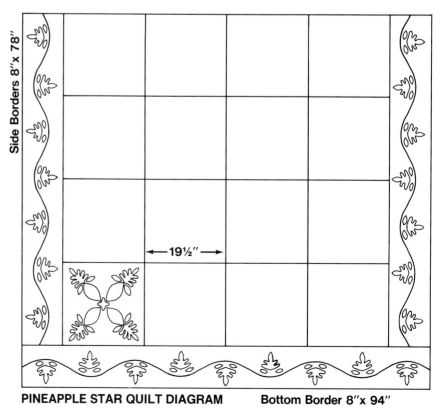

PINEAPPLE STAR QUILT DIAGRAM   **Bottom Border 8"x 94"**

Side Borders 8"x 78"

←— 19½" —→

134

A

C

B

D

E

For Border

PINEAPPLE QUILT PATTERN PIECES

135

To prepare the bias to make the border vine and the stems, fold the remaining bias in thirds, *lengthwise,* to approximately ⅜ inch finished width. Press, then baste through the center of the bias to keep the raw edges tucked under.

TO MAKE ONE BLOCK: To prepare the appliqué pieces, turn under the seam allowances on the marked line and baste.

To determine block center and create placement lines for appliqué pieces, fold a white square in half diagonally and lightly press. Open out square, and fold it in half diagonally the other direction and press.

Referring to photograph, pin appliqué pieces to square, using the diagonal folds as placement guides. Appliqué, using thread colors to match shapes being sewn down.

TO MAKE THE QUILT TOP: Appliqué 16 Pineapple Star blocks.

To assemble quilt top and make borders, refer to quilt diagram on page 134. Measurements on diagram are finished size and do not include seam allowances. Sew blocks into four rows with four blocks in each row. Stitch rows together.

Cut 25 border stems, *each* 2½ inches long, from the folded bias. Prepare the E pieces and the remaining D pieces for appliqué.

To make one side border, measure the length of the quilt top through the center of the quilt, not along the sides, which may have stretched. Mark one side border this length (78½ inches). Referring to the photograph and the quilt diagram on page 134, baste vine bias within the marked border length, forming eight gentle curves along the vine.

Appliqué a stem, two D leaves, and an E piece in each dip of the vine to form a total of eight border flowers. Appliqué the vine in place. Repeat for the other side border.

Check the border length; trim borders to size. Center and sew borders to opposite sides of the quilt top.

To make the bottom border, measure the quilt top, including the two side borders. Mark the length on the bottom border (92½ inches). Baste

the vine along the border, forming nine gentle curves. Appliqué the vine and nine flowers to the border.

Check the border length; trim the border to size. Center and sew the border to the quilt bottom edge.

FINISHING INSTRUCTIONS: Piece the quilt back. Mark the quilt top in a diagonal grid of ¾-inch squares. Layer and baste the quilt back, batting, and quilt top; quilt.

Trim quilt back and batting even with quilt top; round corners slightly. Bind outer edges with green bias.

Country Star Quilt

Shown on pages 130 and 131.
Finished quilt is 74x74 inches.

MATERIALS
3½ yards of muslin
2 yards of red solid fabric
1¾ yards of green print fabric
1¾ yards of red print fabric
5½ yards of fabric for the quilt back
Quilt batting
Cardboard or plastic to make templates

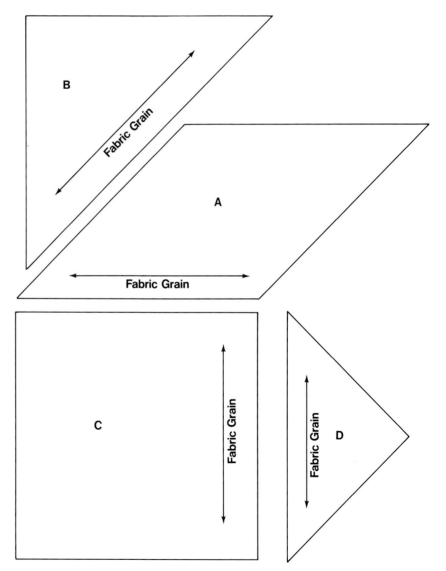

COUNTRY STAR QUILT PATTERN PIECES

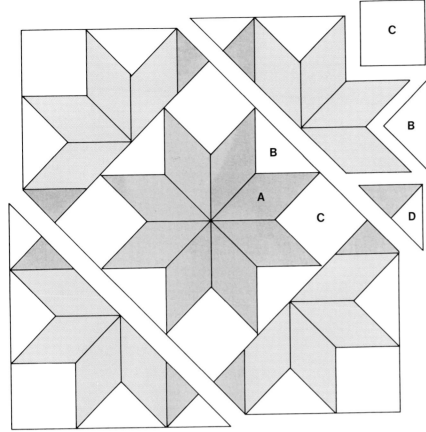

COUNTRY STAR QUILT PIECING DIAGRAM

For two of the half-star units, add a green D triangle along the sides of the two outside diamonds. Stitch these half-stars to *opposite* sides of the center star.

Make four larger triangles by adding a green D triangle to a muslin D triangle. Add these larger triangles to the remaining two half-star units. Sew the half-stars to the remaining sides of center to complete block.

The finished Country Star block should measure 15 inches, including seam allowances.

TO MAKE THE QUILT TOP: Piece 16 Country Star blocks. Sew the blocks into four rows, with four blocks in each row. Join the four rows. The quilt top without borders should measure 58½ inches, including seam allowances.

Center and sew the borders to the quilt top, trimming excess border fabric after the borders are added. Begin by sewing the 3½x62-inch red borders to opposite sides of the quilt top. Stitch the 3½x67-inch red borders to the two remaining sides.

Sew the 5½x67-inch muslin borders to opposite sides of the quilt top. Sew the 5½x77-inch borders to the two remaining sides.

FINISHING INSTRUCTIONS: To piece the quilt back, divide backing fabric into two 2¾-yard lengths. Cut or tear one length in half lengthwise. Sew one half-panel to each side of the full panel, matching the selvage edges and taking a ½-inch seam. Trim selvages, leaving ¼-inch seam margins. Press seams to one side.

Layer the quilt back, batting, and quilt top; baste. Quilt as desired. On the quilt shown in the photograph, the patchwork shapes are outline-quilted ¼ inch from the seams.

When quilting is complete, trim the excess batting and backing fabric even with the quilt top.

Sew the bias binding onto the right side of the quilt. Turn under the raw edge of the binding ¼ inch. Hand-stitch binding to quilt back.

INSTRUCTIONS

Trace and make templates for the patterns, *opposite*. Patterns are finished size; add ¼-inch seam allowances when cutting the pieces from the fabric.

CUTTING INSTRUCTIONS: The number of pieces to cut for the entire quilt is listed first, followed, in parentheses, by the number to cut for one block. Cut all triangular pieces (B and D) with the *long* side of the triangle on the fabric grain.

Cutting measurements for the borders include seam allowances and are longer than is needed. The borders will be trimmed to size when added to the quilt top.

From the muslin, cut two 5½x67-inch borders and two 5½x77-inch borders. From the remaining muslin, cut pieces as follows: 192 (12) of B, 128 (8) of C, and 64 (4) of D.

From the solid red fabric, cut the inner borders. Cut two 3½x62-inch borders and two 3½x67-inch borders. From the remaining red fabric, cut 9 yards of 1½-inch-wide bias for the quilt binding.

From the red print fabric, cut 256 (16) of A.

From the green print fabric, cut 128 (8) of A and 128 (8) of D.

TO PIECE ONE BLOCK: Referring to the piecing diagram, *above,* sew eight green diamonds together to make a star.

Set four B triangles, then four C squares, into the outside of star to form a square.

Sew groups of four red print diamonds into four half-stars. Set two B triangles and one C square into the openings between the diamonds on each half-star.

Kids' Countdown to Christmas

This just-for-kids chapter will help you keep your youngsters occupied in the days before Christmas. Children can count away the days with an Advent calendar, while they create a stocking, cookie puppets, or gift wraps and cards.

Cut from felt and easily stitched with yarn, the dog-shaped stocking, *right,* has room for lots of presents from Santa.

Craft the Advent calendar, *opposite,* from adhesive paper and numbers. Let the kids draw in a "snowstorm" on the background with markers.

Ask your child to design and cut felt decorations to trim the tree. Starting on December 1, replace the highest number with an ornament to count down the days until Christmas.

The cheerful tree of treats below *is a charming invitation to the birds in your neighborhood. Children can make each of the tantalizing trims, then tie them onto branches with red ribbon and string (the bright color attracts birds). Keep the tree filled with goodies all winter so the birds can depend on this food supply when the ground is covered with ice or crusted snow.*

Making cards and decorating packages can be part of the preholiday fun. Suggest simple Christmas symbols such as those shown on the cards *above;* then, let children tear shapes from colorful origami paper. Glue the shapes to construction-paper cards they've cut and folded.

Give children an assortment of festive papers, stickers, and ribbons, and delight in the wrapping ideas they create. See the photograph at *right* for inspiration.

For kids who like to spend time in the kitchen, we have cooked up a recipe for munchable marionettes. Your children can reproduce our Santa and elf characters, or they can use their own imaginations to create a cast of Christmas characters.

While you stir up and chill a large batch of gingerbread dough, have the kids trace the puppet patterns on pages 148 and 149.

Arrange the patterns on rolled-out dough and cut around the shapes with a toothpick, *left*. Poke holes in the body pieces as shown on the patterns. Pull away the excess dough around the puppet pieces.

Cool the cookies, then frost with icing. Join the puppet pieces with pipe cleaners held in place with gumdrops, as shown *above*.

Add colorful strings and crossed slats, and the puppets are ready to perform, *opposite*.

Treats for the Birds
Shown on page 140.

MATERIALS
Cupcake tins
Paper cupcake liners
Wire
Needle
Buttonhole, quilting, or carpet
 thread
Cookie cutters in assorted shapes
Pinecones
Beef suet
Birdseed
Grit
Food as noted in the instructions
 below

INSTRUCTIONS
SUET CAKES: Mix equal parts melted beef suet and sugar syrup (three parts water and one part sugar, boiled together).

While the mixture is soft, add nuts, seeds, bread crumbs, birdseed, grit, or raisins. Spoon the mixture into cupcake tins lined with paper liners and chill the tins in the refrigerator overnight.

Wire the cakes to the tree; store the remaining cakes in the freezer. Replenish the tree with more cakes as needed.

FRUIT TREATS: Poke round orange slices onto branches or cut an orange in half to make a hanging basket. Scoop out the fruit and fill the orange halves with cranberries and raisins. Hang the orange baskets on the tree with wires.

POPCORN GARLANDS: Use the largest variety of popcorn available. Thread a slender needle with a long piece of carpet, buttonhole, or quilting thread.

Thread kernels of popped corn, interspersing the corn with fresh cranberries for color. To tie off the ends of the garlands, loop the thread around the last kernel or two of popcorn before tying knots in thread.

1 Square = 4 Inches

MARSHMALLOW GARLANDS: Thread a slender needle with a long piece of carpet, buttonhole, or quilting thread. To provide sugar for the birds, string garlands of miniature marshmallows, interspersing them with popcorn, chunks of stale bread, carrot slices, or cranberries.

Note: Use stale or dried out marshmallows, because fresh ones will stick to the needle while being threaded or may fall off during the threading process.

BIRD COOKIES: Cut stale bread into holiday shapes such as stars, birds, or trees, using cookie cutters.

Tie the cookies to branches with red string or ribbon.

PEANUT BUTTER PINECONES: Spread pinecones with peanut butter, then roll them in a coating of birdseed and grit.

Fasten each one to a firm branch with a twist of floral wire.

Advent Tree
Shown on page 139.
Finished tree is 33x44 inches.

MATERIALS
33x44-inch bulletin board or white
 foam-core board
White paper to cover the bulletin
 board
2 yards of green, flocked adhesive
 paper
1 yard *each* of red, blue, and
 yellow adhesive paper for
 ornaments
Black permanent marker for
 details
Purchased adhesive numbers from
 1 to 24 (or make your own
 numbers from adhesive paper)
Paper clips

INSTRUCTIONS
If you are using a bulletin board, cover the front with white paper.

Enlarge the tree pattern, *above,* onto large paper.

Use paper clips to clip the pattern to the green flocked paper; cut out the tree. (Piece if necessary.)

Remove the backing and affix the tree to the white background.

Affix numbers to the tree, one for each day from December 1 until Christmas Day.

Draw, then cut out, assorted decorations from red, yellow, and blue adhesive paper. Affix decorations to the tree and background paper. Add details with a black marker.

Dog Stocking
Shown on page 138.
Finished stocking is 13 inches tall.

MATERIALS
15x22-inch piece of light brown felt (stocking)
6x8-inch piece of dark brown felt (ear)
4x6-inch scrap of white felt (muzzle)
Black felt scrap (nose, eye)
½-inch-diameter white button (eye)
3 yards of black knitting worsted yarn
½-inch-diameter white button

INSTRUCTIONS
Trace the pattern on pages 146–147; cut out the pattern pieces. Pin or tape the patterns to felt; cut shapes from felt.

With yarn, stitch French knots on the muzzle. Then glue the muzzle to the stocking front.

Glue the nose to the muzzle. Glue a yarn mouth on the muzzle, and glue yarn around the muzzle edge.

Glue a felt eye on the stocking. Center a button on the felt eye; sew in place.

With a needle threaded with yarn and using running stitches, sew the top of the ear to the stocking top.

With *wrong* sides together and using running stitches, sew the stocking front and back together with yarn, leaving the ear loose at the back edge.

Referring to the photograph on page 138, fashion a fur tuft, and sew it to the stocking top.

Cookie Puppets
Shown on page 142.

INGREDIENTS
Cookie dough
6 cups of flour
1 cup of butter or margarine
2 cups of brown sugar
2 eggs
1 cup of milk
1 teaspoon of vanilla
1 teaspoon of salt
1 teaspoon of baking soda
1 teaspoon of baking powder

Puppet decorating and assembly
Waxed freezer paper
Aluminum foil
Toothpicks
Red, green, white, pink, and chocolate icings
Gumdrops
Four 6-inch-long pipe cleaners for *each* puppet
Six ¼x1x8-inch boards
Colored string
Crafts glue
Frosting decorating bag and tips
Butter knife

INSTRUCTIONS
TO MAKE THE DOUGH: Cream the butter; add the sugar. Beat until fluffy. Add the vanilla and the eggs; mix. Stir in the milk. Sift together the flour, salt, baking soda, and baking powder. Add to other ingredients; mix until thoroughly blended. Cover; freeze for at least 30 minutes.

Trace the patterns on pages 148–149 onto waxed freezer paper. Cut out the pattern pieces.

Refrigerate the extra dough, removing 2 cups of dough at a time for each puppet. (Cold dough is more manageable.)

Place the chilled dough on a sheet of aluminum foil. Roll the dough to ¼-inch thickness.

Arrange the patterns on top of the rolled dough. Cut around the patterns with a toothpick.

Make holes in the dough where indicated on the patterns. Remove excess dough around the pieces. Slide the foil onto a cookie sheet.

Bake in a 400° oven for 10 minutes or until light brown. Let cookies cool before removing.

TO DECORATE THE PUPPETS: Spread colored frosting onto the cookies with a butter knife for the face and clothing. To trim the cookie fronts, squeeze on icings through decorating tips. Add face and clothing lines. Refer to the photograph on page 142 for color ideas.

TO ASSEMBLE THE PUPPETS: Form a small loop in one end of a 6-inch pipe cleaner. Twist the end around the bottom of the loop to secure it.

Thread the straight end of a pipe cleaner from the back through the hole in the shoulder of the arm piece and corresponding shoulder hole in the body.

Position the loop over the hole; pull the straight end up through the loop. Cut off the excess, *leaving at least ½ inch of pipe cleaner for the gumdrop trim.* Push a gumdrop over the end to hold the joint together. Repeat for remaining three joints.

String the puppets by placing the cookies on a flat surface with puppet arms and legs positioned downward. Using square knots, tie one string to the end of each puppet limb and to the hole in the puppet head.

Cut strings so they all extend 12 inches above the puppet head. For extra strength, place a dab of crafts glue on top of the knots.

Drill a hole ½ inch from the end of each stick and another in the middle of each stick. Cross the sticks.

Bring puppet head string through the center stick holes and tie to the upper stick, using a square knot. Bring the arm strings up through the ends of one stick and the leg strings through the other stick. Secure in place with square knots; add crafts glue to the knots. Allow to dry.

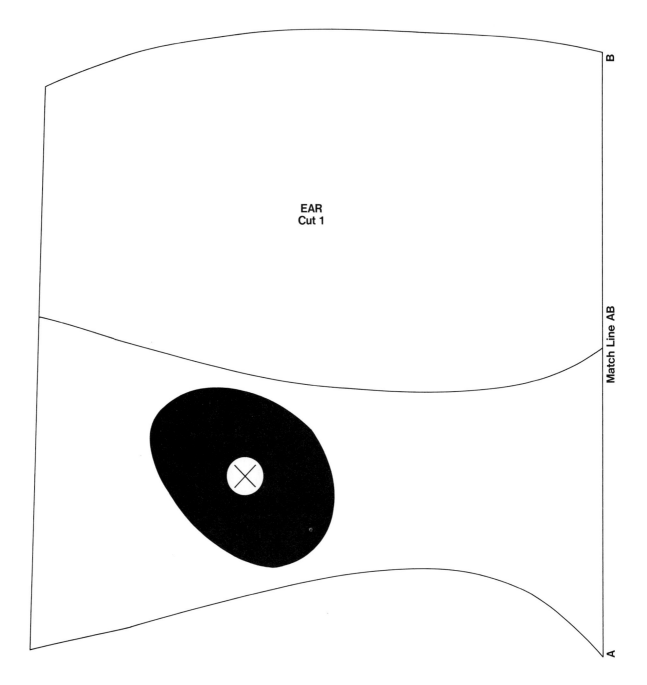

EAR
Cut 1

Match Line AB

B

A

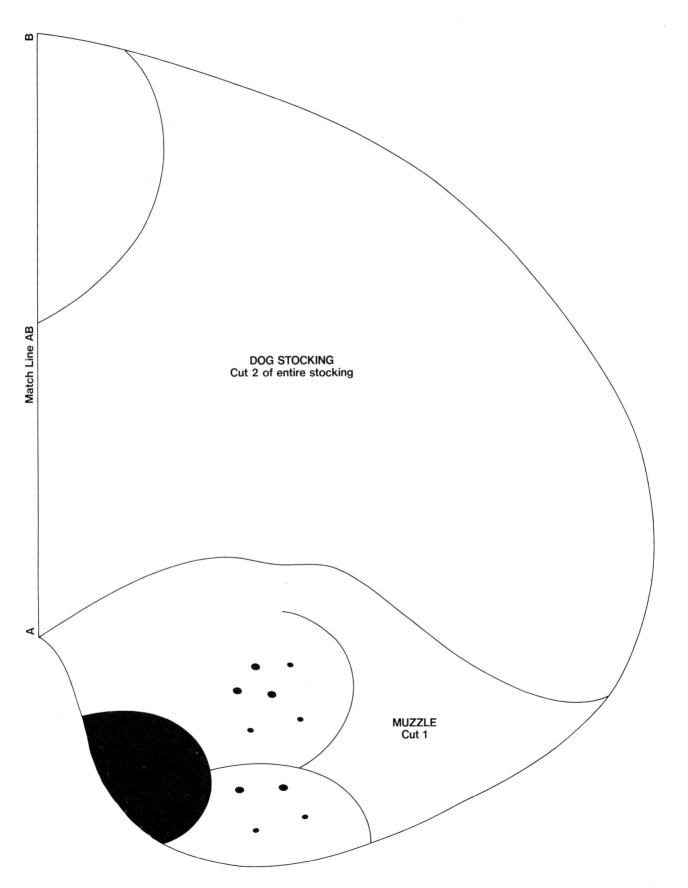

B

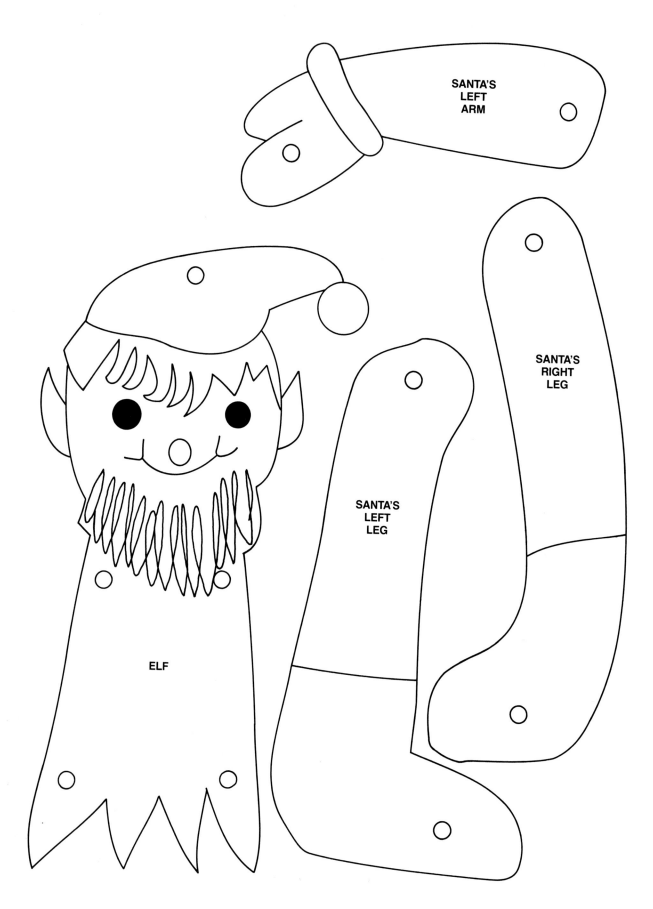

SANTA'S
LEFT
ARM

SANTA'S
RIGHT
LEG

SANTA'S
LEFT
LEG

ELF

SANTA'S
RIGHT
ARM

ELF'S
LEFT
ARM

ELF'S
RIGHT
ARM

ELF'S
RIGHT
LEG

ELF'S
LEFT
LEG

SANTA

Christmas Cherubs

Few things make a holiday merrier than the loving face of a child caught up in the excitement of the season. Handcrafted toys, such as these special dolls, are sure to bring a look of unrestrained delight to your child's face. This angelic pair, dressed in elegant taffeta and lace, is ready for a Christmas party.

If the art of making dolls is a new experience for you, start with dolls like these 22-inch-tall cherubs that are easy to make and sure to charm children.

Their faces are simple to stitch. Cut the eyes from black felt and the cheeks from pink felt; embroider the mouth in backstitches, using red embroidery floss.

Although the elegant and fussy fabrics make the clothing appear complicated, the outfits are easy to sew because they are part of the bodies. You can change the appearance of the dolls simply by dressing them in homespun and calico for a country look.

Instructions for both dolls begin on page 152, with full-size patterns on pages 153–157.

Christmas Angels

*Shown on pages 150 and 151.
Finished dolls are approximately
22 inches tall.*

MATERIALS
Yardages listed are for 45-inch-
  wide fabric

For both angels
⅔ yard of white cotton fabric for
  the legs, wings, and boy's shirt
¼ yard of light peach cotton fabric
  for the faces and hands
3⅔ yards of 1-inch-wide ruffled
  eyelet for the wings, the boy's
  shirt, and the girl's dress sleeves
Off-white yarn for the hair
Scraps of pink felt for the cheeks
Scraps of black felt for the eyes
Red embroidery floss
Polyester fiberfill
Tissue paper
Dressmaker's carbon paper

For the girl
⅓ yard of red moiré taffeta
15 inches of 5-inch-wide ruffled
  eyelet for the apron
1 yard of 1½-inch-wide ruffled
  eyelet for the apron
⅔ yard of ½-inch-wide red satin
  ribbon for hair bows

For the boy
⅓ yard of green moiré taffeta
⅓ yard of ¾-inch-wide green
  ribbon for the bow tie
4 inches of ½-inch-wide
  embroidered eyelet tape for the
  shirt front

INSTRUCTIONS
Trace the full-size patterns on
pages 153–157 onto tissue paper.
Note: The pattern pieces include ¼-
inch seam allowances.

Sew all pieces with right sides
facing unless directed otherwise.

For both dolls
Cut the hands from peach fabric.

From the white fabric, cut the
legs, wings, boy's body top (shirt),
and boy's arms.

Cut the girl's body, arms, and
shoes from red moiré.

Cut the boy's pants and shoes
from green moiré.

HEAD/FACE: Using dressmaker's
carbon, transfer the front head pattern and facial features onto peach
fabric. Do not cut out until the embroidery is complete.

Cut a piece of red embroidery
floss about 12 to 15 inches long. Sep-
arate two strands of floss from the
six strands. Backstitch mouth using
two strands of red embroidery floss.

Cut cheeks from the pink felt; cut
eyes from the black felt. Whipstitch
eyes and cheeks in place.

Cut out the head fronts and head
backs from peach fabric. Sew together, leaving an opening at top.

Clip the curves, turn to the right
side, and press.

Stuff the heads with fiberfill and
slip-stitch the opening closed.

SHOES/LEGS: Turn under the top
edge of the shoes, clipping curves as
necessary. Topstitch the shoes to
the legs.

Sew the legs together in pairs,
leaving the tops open for turning.
Clip the curves, turn to the right side,
and press.

Stuff the legs firmly with polyester fiberfill. Baste the leg tops together; set aside.

Girl angel
BODY: Sew the legs to the front
body piece. Pin the legs upward
onto the body piece to hold them in
place and out of the way.

Sew the body pieces together,
leaving an opening at the top for
turning right side out.

Clip the curves, turn to the right
side, and press. Stuff firmly with
polyester fiberfill. Slip-stitch the
opening closed.

Sew the head firmly in place atop
the body.

HANDS/ARMS: Baste 1-inch-wide
eyelet to the straight edges of the

arm pieces (dress sleeves). Sew the
hands to the arms, catching the eyelet in the seam.

Stitch the hand/arm pieces together in pairs, leaving an opening
at the top.

Clip the curves, turn to the right
side, and press.

Stuff with polyester fiberfill and
slip-stitch the opening closed. Stitch
finger lines in the hands.

Sew the arms to the shoulders.

WINGS: Baste 1-inch-wide eyelet
along the seam line on the right side
of two of the wing pieces.

Sew the wing pieces together in
pairs, catching the eyelet in the
seam and leaving an opening for
turning right side out.

Clip the curves and points; turn to
the right side. Press, then stuff lightly. Turn under the raw edges and
slip-stitch the opening closed.

Quilt wings if desired; set aside.

HAIR: Wrap yarn 40 times around a
14-inch length of cardboard. Carefully slip the yarn from the cardboard and machine-stitch across the
middle to form a part.

Sew the hair to the head at the
part. Tie the hair into pigtails.

Tie a red ribbon bow around each
pigtail; tack in place.

APRON: Position the bottom scalloped edge of the apron eyelet atop
the 1½-inch-wide eyelet trim; stitch
in place.

Press under ¼ inch twice on the
short sides of the apron; hem.

Cut two 7-inch lengths of 1½-
inch-wide eyelet for apron straps.

Locate the center of the apron at
the waist. Pin the straight edge of
the eyelet lengths 1 inch from the
waistband center on each side;
stitch the ends of the eyelet to the
apron waist.

Cross the lengths in back and sew
the ends to the back of the apron at
the waist.

Slip the apron onto the angel and
tack in place.

Sew the wings to the body.

Boy angel

BODY: Baste two 4-inch lengths of 1-inch-wide ruffled eyelet to both sides of the embroidered tape; stitch in place. Sew the tape to the center front of the body top (shirt front).

Sew the shirt pieces to pants tops.

Sew the legs to the pant legs. Pin the legs upward onto the pants to hold them out of the way.

Sew the shirt/pants pieces together, leaving an opening at the top for turning right side out.

Clip the curves, turn to the right side, and press. Stuff firmly with polyester fiberfill, and slip-stitch the opening closed.

Center the head atop the body. Sew the head firmly in place.

HANDS/ARMS: Sew the hands to the arms.

Stitch the hand/arm pieces together in pairs, leaving an opening at the top for turning.

Clip the curves, turn to the right side, and press. Stuff firmly with polyester fiberfill, and slip-stitch the opening closed.

Stitch finger lines in hands either on the sewing machine or with running stitches by hand.

Sew the arms to the shoulders.

WINGS: Sew the wing pieces together in pairs, leaving an opening for turning.

Clip curves and points and turn to the right side. Press, then stuff lightly with polyester fiberfill.

Turn under the raw edges and slip-stitch the opening closed.

Pin 1-inch-wide ruffled eyelet to the wings 3 inches from the scalloped edge, turning under the raw edges. Stitch in place.

Tack the wings to the back of the boy's shirt.

HAIR: Wrap yarn around an 8-inch length of cardboard 25 times. Tie the yarn 3 inches from one end to form a side part. Slip yarn off cardboard.

Sew the yarn to the doll's head.

Tie the green ribbon into a bow; securely tack it to the shirt front.

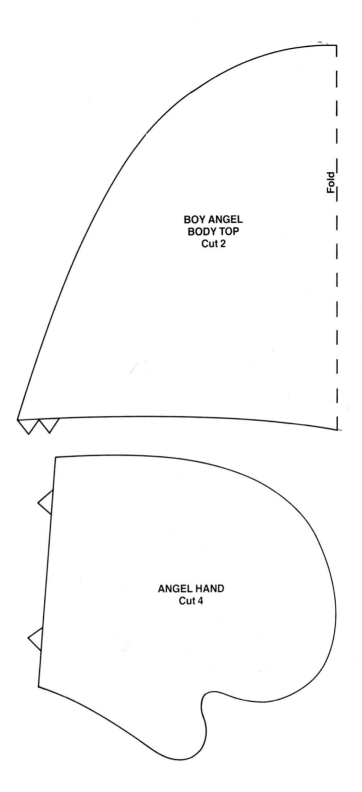

BOY ANGEL
BODY TOP
Cut 2

Fold

ANGEL HAND
Cut 4

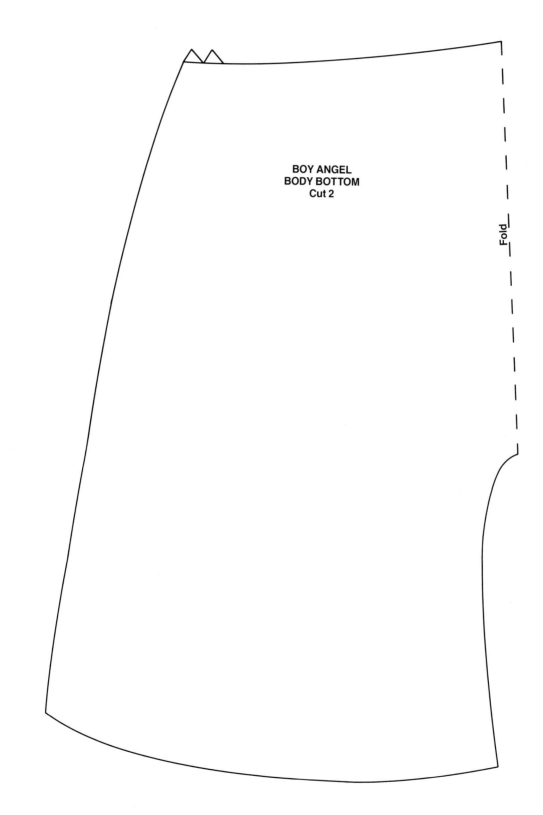

BOY ANGEL
BODY BOTTOM
Cut 2

Fold

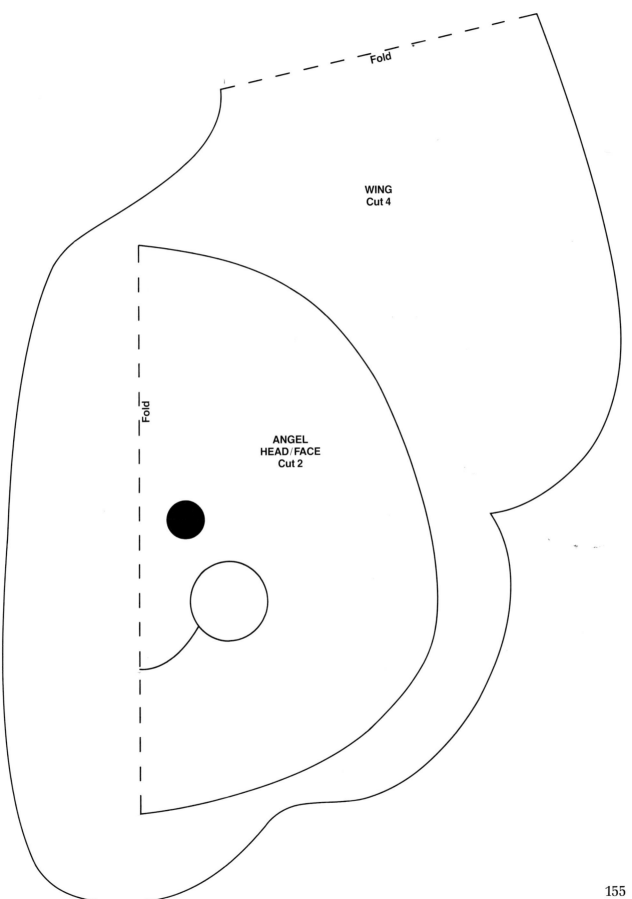

WING
Cut 4

Fold

Fold

ANGEL
HEAD / FACE
Cut 2

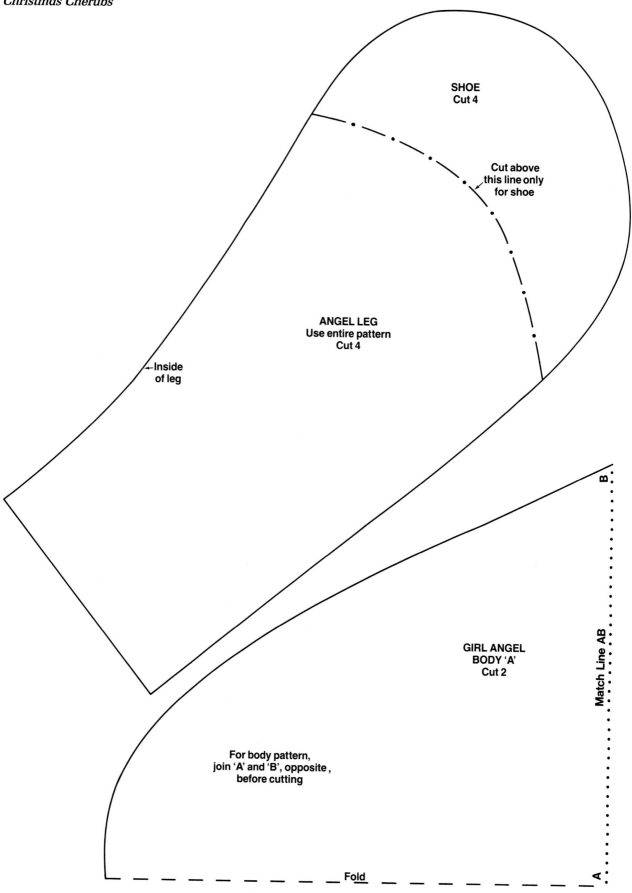

SHOE
Cut 4

Cut above
this line only
for shoe

←Inside
of leg

ANGEL LEG
Use entire pattern
Cut 4

B

GIRL ANGEL
BODY 'A'
Cut 2

Match Line AB

For body pattern,
join 'A' and 'B', opposite,
before cutting

A

Fold

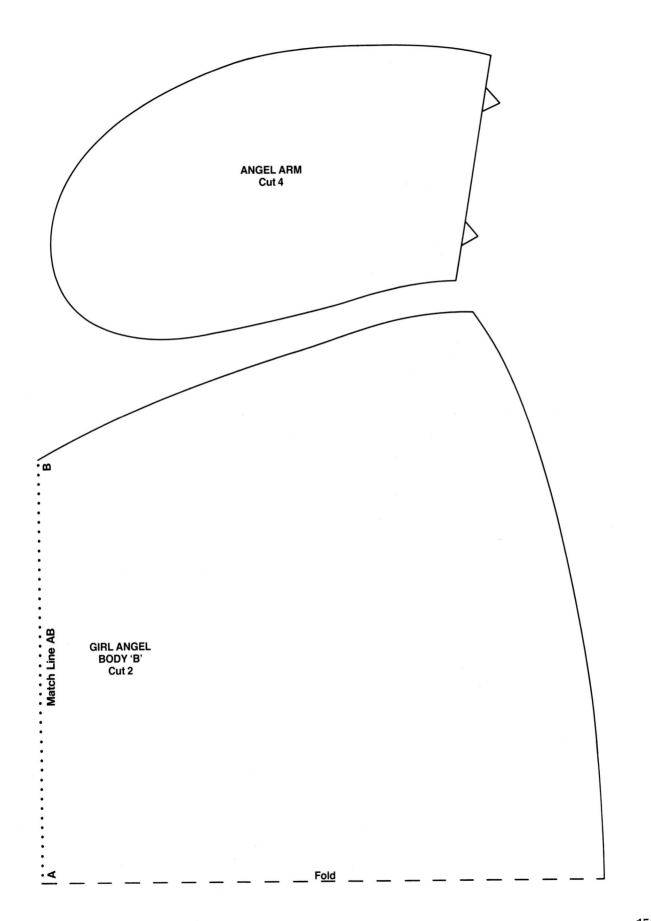

ANGEL ARM
Cut 4

GIRL ANGEL
BODY 'B'
Cut 2

B

Match Line AB

A

Fold

CREDITS

We would like to express our gratitude and appreciation to the many people who helped with this book.

Our heartfelt thanks go to each of the artists and designers, who so enthusiastically contributed ideas, designs, and projects.

Thanks also to the photographers, whose creative talents and technical skills added much to the book.

We are happy as well to acknowledge our indebtedness to the many companies, collectors, needlecrafters, and others who generously shared their stitched pieces and projects with us, or in some other way contributed to the production of this book.

Designers

Beth Bohac—33, place mats
Gary Boling—11
Coats and Clark—122
Joan Cravens—82–83, ornament; 84–85, stockings
Phyllis Dunstan—14–15, goat family
Dixie Falls—17, knit stockings; 68
Verna Fuller—120–121, ornaments
Gloria Hander—102, angel and ornaments
Janet Harrington—17, fireboard and crewel pillows

Adam Jerdee—139, tree
Amy Jerdee—140
Rebecca Jerdee—6–10; 33, pot holders; 34, wreath; 36–37, child's furniture and lace ornaments; 38–39, quilt ornaments and doll quilts; 64–65, twig stars
Susan Knight—12–13, pillow; 16

Judy LaSalle—150–151
Carol Lisboa—110–111
Salley Mavor—37, doll; 69
Sandi Moran—35; 98–99

David Reep (for Hallmark Cards)—141, gift wrap
Abby Ruoff—64–65, chairs and candlesticks; 67, frame
Ed Sibbett, Jr.—114–115
Becky Smith—138; 139, tree decorations; 141, cards
Rhoda Sneller—84–85, stockings and album

Ciba Vaughan—67, velvet stars
Judy Veeder—82–83, place mats and runner
Susan Welsh—33, rag baskets
Jim Williams—12–13, picket fence; 15, miniature picket fence; 36–37, rag ornaments; 54–55; 66
James Yocum (for Valley Hill Herbs and Everlastings)—102–103, crèche

Photographers

Sean Fitzgerald—130–131
Jim Hedrich—10; 102–103, crèche
Thomas Hooper—12–17; 64–69
Hopkins Associates—6–9; 102, angel and ornaments; 120–123; 132–133
Michael Jensen—80–85
Scott Little—11; 98–99; 110–111; 114–115; 138–143; 150–151
Perry Struse—32–39; 54–55

Acknowledgments

Margaret Cavigga

C.M. Offray and Son, Inc.
261 Madison Ave.
New York, NY 10016

Coats and Clark, Inc.
72 Cummings Rd.
Stamford, CT 06904

DMC Corporation
197 Trumbull St.
Elizabeth, NJ 07206

Marianne Fons

Alta Glen

Hallmark Cards, Inc.
2501 McGee
Kansas City, MO 64108

Marie Holmstrand

Gail Kinkead

Murphy's Landing
Shakopee, MN 55379

INDEX

Page numbers in **bold** type indicate photographs; remaining page numbers refer to how-to instructions and patterns.

INDEX